SALT-WATER
POEMS AND BALLADS

"Lord, what a handsome ship she be
Cheer her, sonny boys, three time three!"
And the dockside loafers gave her a shout
As the red-funneled tugboat towed her out.

SALT-WATER
POEMS AND BALLADS

BY

JOHN MASEFIELD

ILLUSTRATED BY
CHAS. PEARS

THE MACMILLAN COMPANY, PUBLISHERS,
NEW YORK   MCMLXV

CONTENTS

SALT–WATER BALLADS

CONTENTS

SALT–WATER BALLADS

A CONSECRATION

NOT of the princes and prelates with periwigged charioteers
Riding triumphantly laurelled to lap the fat of the years, —
Rather the scorned — the rejected — the men hemmed in
*   with the spears;*

The men of the tattered battalion which fights till it dies,
Dazed with the dust of the battle, the din and the cries,
The men with the broken heads and the blood running into
*   their eyes.*

Not the be-medalled Commander, beloved of the throne,
Riding cock-horse to parade when the bugles are blown,
But the lads who carried the koppie and cannot be known.

Not the ruler for me, but the ranker, the tramp of the road,
The slave with the sack on his shoulders pricked on with the
*   goad,*
The man with too weighty a burden, too weary a load.

The sailor, the stoker of steamers, the man with the clout,
The chantyman bent at the halliards putting a tune to the
*   shout,*
The drowsy man at the wheel and the tired lookout.

3

Others may sing of the wine and the wealth and the mirth,
The portly presence of potentates goodly in girth; —
Mine be the dirt and the dross, the dust and scum of the
    earth !

THEIRS *be the music, the colour, the glory, the gold;*
Mine be a handful of ashes, a mouthful of mould.
Of the maimed, of the halt and the blind in the rain and the
    cold —

Of these shall my songs be fashioned, my tales be told.

AMEN.

THE YARN OF THE 'LOCH ACHRAY'

THE 'Loch Achray' was a clipper tall
With seven-and-twenty hands in all.
Twenty to hand and reef and haul,
A skipper to sail and mates to bawl
'Tally on to the tackle-fall,
Heave now 'n' start her, heave 'n' pawl!'
  Hear the yarn of a sailor,
  An old yarn learned at sea.

Her crew were shipped and they said 'Farewell,
So-long, my Tottie, my lovely gell;
We sail to-day if we fetch to hell,
It's time we tackled the wheel a spell.'
  Hear the yarn of a sailor,
  An old yarn learned at sea.

The dockside loafers talked on the quay
The day that she towed down to sea:
'Lord, what a handsome ship she be!
Cheer her, sonny boys, three times three!'
And the dockside loafers gave her a shout
As the red-funnelled tug-boat towed her out;
They gave her a cheer as the custom is,
And the crew yelled 'Take our loves to Liz —

5

Three cheers, bullies, for old Pier Head
'N' the bloody stay-at-homes!' they said.
    Hear the yarn of a sailor,
    An old yarn learned at sea.

In the grey of the coming on of night
She dropped the tug at the Tuskar Light,
'N' the topsails went to the topmast head
To a chorus that fairly awoke the dead.
She trimmed her yards and slanted South
With her royals set and a bone in her mouth.
    Hear the yarn of a sailor,
    An old yarn learned at sea.

She crossed the Line and all went well,
They ate, they slept, and they struck the bell
And I give you a gospel truth when I state
The crowd didn't find any fault with the Mate,
But one night off the River Plate.
    Hear the yarn of a sailor,
    An old yarn learned at sea.

It freshened up till it blew like thunder
And burrowed her deep, lee-scuppers under.
The old man said, 'I mean to hang on
Till her canvas busts or her sticks are gone' —
Which the blushing looney did, till at last
Overboard went her mizzen-mast.
    Hear the yarn of a sailor,
    An old yarn learned at sea.

Then a fierce squall struck the 'Loch Achray'
And bowed her down to her water-way;
Her main-shrouds gave and her forestay,
And a green sea carried her wheel away;
Ere the watch below had time to dress
She was cluttered up in a blushing mess.
        Hear the yarn of a sailor,
        An old yarn learned at sea.

She couldn't lay-to nor yet pay-off,
And she got swept clean in the bloody trough;
Her masts were gone, and afore you knowed
She filled by the head and down she goed.
Her crew made seven-and-twenty dishes
For the big jack-sharks and the little fishes,
And over their bones the water swishes.
        Hear the yarn of a sailor,
        An old yarn learned at sea.

The wives and girls they watch in the rain
For a ship as won't come home again.
'I reckon it's them head-winds,' they say,
'She'll be home to-morrow, if not to-day.
I'll just nip home 'n' I'll air the sheets
'N' buy the fixins 'n' cook the meats
As my man likes 'n' as my man eats.'

So home they goes by the windy streets,
Thinking their men are homeward bound

With anchors hungry for English ground,
And the bloody fun of it is, they're drowned!
    Hear the yarn of a sailor,
    An old yarn learned at sea.

SING A SONG O' SHIPWRECK

HE lolled on a bollard, a sun-burned son of the sea,
With ear-rings of brass and a jumper of dungaree,
''N' many a queer lash-up have I seen,' says he.

'But the toughest hooray o' the racket,' he says, 'I'll
   be sworn,
'N' the roughest traverse I worked since the day I was
   born,
Was a packet o' Sailor's Delight as I scoffed in the seas
   o' the Horn.

'All day long in the calm she had rolled to the swell,
Rolling through fifty degrees till she clattered her bell;
'N' then came snow, 'n' a squall, 'n' a wind was colder
   'n hell.

'It blew like the Bull of Barney, a beast of a breeze,
'N' over the rail come the cold green lollopin' seas,
'N' she went ashore at the dawn on the Ramirez.

'She was settlin' down by the stern when I got to the
   deck,
Her waist was a smother o' sea as was up to your neck,
'N' her masts were gone, 'n' her rails, 'n' she was a wreck.

9

'We rigged up a tackle, a purchase, a sort of a shift,
To hoist the boats off o' the deck-house and get them
    adrift,
When her stern gives a sickenin' settle, her bows give a
    lift,

"'N' comes a crash of green water as sets me afloat
With freezing fingers clutching the keel of a boat —
The bottom-up whaler — 'n' that was the juice of a
    note.

'Well, I clambers acrost o' the keel 'n' I gets me secured,
When I sees a face in the white o' the smother to looard,
So I gives 'im a 'and, 'n' be shot if it wasn't the stooard!

'So he climbs up forrard o' me, 'n' "thanky," a' says,
'N' we sits 'n' shivers 'n' freeze to the bone wi' the sprays,
'N' I sings "Abel Brown," 'n' the stooard he prays.

'Wi' never a dollop to sup nor a morsel to bite,
The lips of us blue with the cold 'n' the heads of us
    light,
Adrift in a Cape Horn sea for a day 'n' a night.

"'N' then the stooard goes dotty 'n' puts a tune to his
    lip,
'N' moans about Love like a dern old hen wi' the pip —
(I sets no store upon stooards — they ain't no use on a
    ship).

'Well, I clambers acrost o' the keel 'n' I gets me secured,
When I sees a face in the white o' the smother to looard,
So I gives 'im a 'and, 'n' be shot if it wasn't the stooard!'

"'N' "mother," the looney cackles, "come 'n' put Willy
  to bed!"
So I says "Dry up, or I'll fetch you a crack o' the head";
"The kettle's a-bilin'," he answers, "'n' I'll go butter
  the bread."

"'N' he falls to singin' some slush about clinkin' a can,
'N' at last he dies, so he does, 'n' I tells you, Jan,
I was glad when he did, for he weren't no fun for a man.

'So he falls forrard, he does, 'n' he closes his eye,
'N' quiet he lays 'n' quiet I leaves him lie,
'N' I was alone with his corp, 'n' the cold green sea and
  the sky.

"'N' then I dithers, I guess, for the next as I knew
Was the voice of a mate as was sayin' to one of the crew,
"Easy, my son, wi' the brandy, be shot if he ain't
  comin'-to!"'

BURIAL PARTY

'HE's deader 'n nails,' the fo'c's'le said, ''n' gone to his
    long sleep';
''N' about his corp,' said Tom to Dan, 'd'ye think his
    corp'll keep
Till the day's done, 'n' the work's through, 'n' the ebb's
    upon the neap?'

'He's deader 'n nails,' said Dan to Tom, ''n' I wish his
    sperrit j'y;
He spat straight 'n' he steered true, but listen to me,
    say I,
Take 'n' cover 'n' bury him now, 'n' I'll take 'n' tell
    you why.

'It's a rummy rig of a guffy's yarn, 'n' the juice of a
    rummy note,
But if you buries a corp at night, it takes 'n' keeps afloat,
For its bloody soul's afraid o' the dark 'n' sticks within
    the throat.

''N' all the night till the grey o' the dawn the dead 'un has
    to swim
With a blue 'n' beastly Will o' the Wisp a-burnin' over
    him,

With a herring, maybe, a-scoffin' a toe or a shark a-chew-
  in' a limb.

"'N' all the night the shiverin' corp it has to swim the
    sea,
With its shudderin' soul inside the throat (where a soul's
    no right to be),
Till the sky's grey 'n' the dawn's clear, 'n' then the sperrit's
    free.

'Now Joe was a man was right as rain.   I'm sort of sore
    for Joe,
'N' if we bury him durin' the day, his soul can take 'n'
    go;
So we'll dump his corp when the bell strikes 'n' we can
    get below.

'I'd fairly hate for him to swim in a blue 'n' beastly
    light,
With his shudderin' soul inside of him a-feelin' the fishes
    bite,
So over he goes at noon, say I, 'n' he shall sleep to-night.'

BILL

He lay dead on the cluttered deck and stared at the cold
    skies,
With never a friend to mourn for him nor a hand to close
    his eyes :
'Bill, he's dead,' was all they said; 'he's dead, 'n' there
    he lies.'

The mate came forrard at seven bells and spat across the
    rail :
'Just lash him up wi' some holystone in a clout o' rotten
    sail,
'N', rot ye, get a gait on ye, ye're slower'n a bloody snail !'

When the rising moon was a copper disc and the sea was
    a strip of steel,
We dumped him down to the swaying weeds ten fathom
    beneath the keel.
'It's rough about Bill,' the fo'c's'le said, 'we'll have to
    stand his wheel.'

FEVER SHIP

THERE'LL be no weepin' gells ashore when *our* ship sails,
Nor no crews cheerin' us, standin' at the rails,
'N' no Blue Peter a-foul the royal stay,
For we've the Yellow Fever — Harry died to-day. —
    It's cruel when a fo'c's'le gets the fever!

'N' Dick has got the fever-shakes, 'n' look what I was told
(I went to get a sack for him to keep him from the cold):
'Sir, can I have a sack?' I says, 'for Dick 'e's fit to die.'
'Oh, sack be shot!' the skipper says, 'jest let the rotter
    lie!' —
    It's cruel when a fo'c's'le gets the fever!

It's a cruel port is Santos, and a hungry land,
With rows o' graves already dug in yonder strip of sand,
'N' Dick is hollerin' up the hatch, 'e says 'e's goin' blue,
His pore teeth are chattering, 'n' what's a man to do? —
    It's cruel when a fo'c's'le gets the fever!

FEVER-CHILLS

HE tottered out of the alleyway with cheeks the colour
   of paste,
And shivered a spell and mopped his brow with a clout
   of cotton waste:
'I've a lick of fever-chills,' he said, ''n' my inside it's
   green,
But I'd be as right as rain,' he said, 'if I had some
   quinine, —
   But there ain't no quinine for us poor sailor-men.

'But them there passengers,' he said, 'if they gets fever-
   chills,
There's brimmin' buckets o' quinine for them, 'n' bulgin'
   crates o' pills,
'N' a doctor with Latin 'n' drugs 'n' all — enough to
   sink a town,
'N' they lies quiet in their blushin' bunks 'n' mops their
   gruel down, —
   But there ain't none o' them fine ways for us poor sailor-
   men.

'But the Chief comes forrard 'n' he says, says he, "I give
   you a straight tip:

He tottered out of the alleyway with cheeks the colour of
        paste,
And shivered a spell and mopped his brow with a clout of
        cotton waste :
'I've a lick of fever-chills,' he said, ' 'n' my inside it's green,
But I'd be as right as rain,' he said, ' if I had some quinine, —
But there ain't no quinine for us poor sailor-men.'

Come none o' your Cape Horn fever lays aboard o' this
    yer ship.
On wi' your rags o' duds, my son, 'n' aft, 'n' down the
    hole :
The best cure known for fever-chills is shovelling bloody
    coal."
    It's *hard*, my son, that's what it is, for us poor sailor‐
    men.'

ONE OF THE BO'SUN'S YARNS

LOAFIN' around in Sailor Town, a-bluin' o' my advance,
I met a derelict donkeyman who led me a merry dance,
Till he landed me 'n' bleached me fair in the bar of a
rum-saloon,
'N' there he spun me a juice of a yarn to this-yer brand
of tune.

'It's a solemn gospel, mate,' he says, 'but a man as ships
aboard
A steamer-tramp, he gets his whack of the wonders of
the Lord —
Such as roaches crawlin' over his bunk, 'n' snakes inside
his bread,
And work by night and work by day enough to strike
him dead.

'But that there's by the way,' says he; 'the yarn I'm
goin' to spin
Is about myself 'n' the life I led in the last ship I was in,
The "Esmeralda," casual tramp, from Hull towards the
Hook,
Wi' one o' the brand o' Cain for mate 'n' a human mis-
take for cook.

'We'd a week or so of dippin' around in a wind from
    outer hell,
With a fathom or more of broken sea at large in the
    forrard well,
Till our boats were bashed and bust and broke and gone
    to Davy Jones,
'N' then come white Atlantic fog as chilled us to the
    bones.

'We slowed her down and started the horn and watch
    and watch about,
We froze the marrow in all our bones a-keepin' a good
    look-out,
'N' the ninth night out, in the middle watch, I woke from
    a pleasant dream,
With the smash of a steamer ramming our plates a point
    abaft the beam.

'"Twas cold and dark when I fetched the deck, dirty
    'n' cold 'n' thick,
'N' there was a feel in the way she rode as fairly turned
    me sick ; —
She was settlin', listin' quickly down, 'n' I heard the
    mates a-cursin',
'N' I heard the wash 'n' the grumble-grunt of a steamer's
    screws reversin'.

'She was leavin' us, mate, to sink or swim, 'n' the words
    we took 'n' said

They turned the port-light grassy-green 'n' the starboard
 rosy-red.
We give her a hot perpetual taste of the singeing curse of
 Cain,
As we heard her back 'n' clear the wreck 'n' off to her
 course again.

'Then the mate came dancin' on to the scene, 'n' he says,
 "Now quit yer chin,
Or I'll smash yer skulls, so help me James, 'n' let some
 wisdom in.
Ye dodderin' scum o' the slums," he says, "are ye drunk
 or blazin' daft?
If ye wish to save yer sickly hides, ye'd best contrive
 a raft."

'So he spoke us fair and turned us to, 'n' we wrought
 wi' tooth and nail
Wi' scantling, casks, 'n' coops 'n' ropes, 'n' boiler-plates
 'n' sail,
'N' all the while it were dark 'n' cold 'n' dirty as it could
 be,
'N' she was soggy 'n' settlin' down to a berth beneath
 the sea.

'Soggy she grew, 'n' she didn't lift, 'n' she listed more
 'n' more,
Till her bell struck 'n' her boiler-pipes began to wheeze
 'n' snore;

She settled, settled, listed, heeled, 'n' then may I be cust,
If her sneezin', wheezin' boiler-pipes did not begin to
    bust!

"N' then the stars began to shine, 'n' the birds began to
    sing,
'N' the next I knowed I was bandaged up 'n' my arm were
    in a sling,
'N' a swab in uniform were there, 'n' "Well," says he,
    "'n' how
Are yer arms, 'n' legs, 'n' liver, 'n' lungs, 'n' bones a-feelin'
    now ?"

"'Where am I ?" says I, 'n' he says, says he, a-cantin'
    to the roll,
"You're aboard the R.M.S. 'Marie' in the after Glory-
    Hole,
'N' you've had a shave, if you wish to know, from the
    port o' Kingdom Come.
Drink this," he says, 'n' I takes 'n' drinks, 'n' s'elp me,
    it was rum!

'Seven survivors seen 'n' saved of the "Esmeralda's"
    crowd,
Taken aboard the sweet "Marie" 'n' bunked 'n' treated
    proud,
'N' D.B.S.'d to Mersey Docks ('n' a joyful trip we made),
'N' there the skipper were given a purse by a grateful
    Board of Trade.

'That's the end o' the yarn,' he says, 'n' he takes 'n'
    wipes his lips,
'Them's the works o' the Lord you sees in steam 'n'
    sailin' ships, —
Rocks 'n' fogs 'n' shatterin' seas 'n' breakers right ahead,
'N' work o' nights 'n' work o' days enough to strike you
    dead.'

HELL'S PAVEMENT

'WHEN I'm discharged in Liverpool 'n' draws my bit o'
    pay,
  I won't come to sea no more.
I'll court a pretty little lass 'n' have a weddin' day,
  'N' settle somewhere down ashore.
I'll never fare to sea again a-temptin' Davy Jones,
A-hearkening to the cruel sharks a-hungerin' for my
    bones ;
I'll run a blushin' dairy-farm or go a-crackin' stones,
  Or buy 'n' keep a little liquor-store,' —
                  So he said.

They towed her in to Liverpool, we made the hooker
    fast,
  And the copper-bound officials paid the crew,
And Billy drew his money, but the money didn't last,
  For he painted the alongshore blue, —
It was rum for Poll, and rum for Nan, and gin for Jolly
    Jack.
He shipped a week later in the clothes upon his back,
He had to pinch a little straw, he had to beg a sack
  To sleep on, when his watch was through, —
                  So he did.

SEA–CHANGE

Goneys an' gullies an' all o' the birds o' the sea,
    They ain't no birds, not really,' said Billy the Dane.
'Not mollies, nor gullies, nor goneys at all,' said he,
    'But simply the sperrits of mariners livin' again.

'Them birds goin' fishin' is nothin' but souls o' the
    drowned,
    Souls o' the drowned an' the kicked as are never no
    more;
An' that there haughty old albatross cruisin' around,
    Belike he's Admiral Nelson or Admiral Noah.

'An' merry's the life they are living. They settle and
    dip,
    They fishes, they never stands watches, they waggle
    their wings;
When a ship comes by, they fly to look at the ship
    To see how the nowaday mariners manages things.

'When freezing aloft in a snorter, I tell you I wish —
    (Though maybe it ain't like a Christian) — I wish I
    could be
A haughty old copper-bound albatross dipping for fish
    And coming the proud over all o' the birds o' the sea.'

26

'Goneys an' gullies an' all o' the birds o' the sea,
 They ain't no birds, not really,' said Billy the Dane.
'Not mollies, nor gullies, nor goneys at all,' said he,
 'But simply the sperrits of mariners livin' again.

'Them birds goin' fishin' is nothin' but souls o' the drowned,
 Souls o' the drowned an' the kicked as are never no more ;
An' that there haughty old albatross cruisin' around,
 Belike he's Admiral Nelson or Admiral Noah.'

HARBOUR BAR

ALL in the feathered palm-tree tops the bright green
    parrots screech,
The white line of the running surf goes booming down the
    beach,
But I shall never see them, though the land lies close
    aboard,
I've shaped the last long silent tack as takes one to the
    Lord.

Give me the Scripters, Jakey, 'n' my pipe atween my lips,
I'm bound for somewhere south and far beyond the track
    of ships;
I've run my rags of colours up and clinched them to the
    stay,
And God the pilot's come aboard to bring me up the bay.

You'll mainsail-haul my bits o' things when Christ has
    took my soul,
'N' you'll lay me quiet somewhere at the landward end
    the Mole,
Where I shall hear the steamers' sterns a-squattering
    from the heave,
And the topsail blocks a-piping when a rope-yarn fouls
    the sheave.

Give me a sup of lime juice; Lord, I'm drifting in to
    port,
The landfall lies to windward and the wind comes light
    and short,
And I'm for signing off and out to take my watch below,
And — prop a fellow, Jakey — Lord, it's time for me to
    go!

THE TURN OF THE TIDE

An' Bill can have my sea-boots, Nigger Jim can have
    my knife,
    You can divvy up the dungarees an' bed,
An' the ship can have my blessing, an' the Lord can have
    my life,
    An' sails an' fish my body when I'm dead.

An' dreaming down below there in the tangled greens an'
    blues,
    Where the sunlight shudders golden round about,
I shall hear the ships complainin' an' the cursin' of the
    crews,
    An' be sorry when the watch is tumbled out.

I shall hear them hilly-hollying the weather crojick brace,
    And the sucking of the wash about the hull;
When they chanty up the topsail I'll be hauling in my
    place,
    For my soul will follow seawards like a gull.

I shall hear the blocks a-grunting in the bumpkins over-
    side,
    An' the slatting of the storm-sails on the stay,
An' the rippling of the catspaw at the making of the tide,
    An' the swirl and splash of porpoises at play.

I shall hear the blocks a-grunting in the bumpkins overside,
   An' the slatting of the storm-sails on the stay,
An' the rippling of the catspaw at the making of the tide,
   An' the swirl and splash of porpoises at play.

An' Bill can have my sea-boots, Nigger Jim can have my
    knife,
  You can divvy up the whack I haven't scofft,
An' the ship can have my blessing and the Lord can have
    my life,
  For it's time I quit the deck and went aloft.

ONE OF WALLY'S YARNS

THE watch was up on the topsail-yard a-making fast the
    sail,
'N' Joe was swiggin' his gasket taut, 'n' I felt the stirrup
    give,
'N' he dropped sheer from the tops'l-yard 'n' barely
    cleared the rail,
'N' o' course, we bein' aloft, *we* couldn't do nothin' —
We couldn't lower a boat and go a-lookin' for him,
For it blew hard 'n' there was sech a sea runnin'
       That no boat wouldn't live.

I seed him rise in the white o' the wake, I seed him lift
    a hand
('N' him in his oilskin suit 'n' all), I heard him lift a cry;
'N' there was his place on the yard 'n' all, 'n' the stirrup's
    busted strand.
'N' the old man said there's a cruel old sea runnin',
A cold green Barney's Bull of a sea runnin';
It's hard, but I ain't agoin' to let a boat be lowered:
       So we left him there to die.

He couldn't have kept afloat for long an' him lashed up
    'n' all,

The watch was up on the topsail-yard a-making fast the sail,
'N' Joe was swiggin' his gasket taut, 'n' I felt the stirrup *give*,
'N' he dropped sheer from the tops'l-yard 'n' barely cleared the rail,
'N' o' course, we bein' aloft, *we* couldn't do nothin' —
We couldn't lower a boat and go a-lookin' for him,
For it blew hard 'n' there was sech a sea runnin'
        That no boat wouldn't live.

'N' we couldn't see him for long, for the sea was blurred
    with the sleet 'n' snow,
'N' we couldn't think of him much because o' the snortin',
    screamin' squall.
There was a hand less at the halliards 'n' the braces,
'N' a name less when the watch spoke to the muster-roll,
'N' a empty bunk 'n' a pannikin as wasn't wanted
    When the watch went below.

A VALEDICTION (LIVERPOOL DOCKS)

A CRIMP.   A DRUNKEN SAILOR.

Is there anything as I can do ashore for you
When you've dropped down the tide? —

You can take 'n' tell Nan I'm goin' about the world agen,
    'N' that the world's wide.
'N' tell her that there ain't no postal service
    Not down on the blue sea.
'N' tell her that she'd best not keep her fires alight
    Nor set up late for me.
'N' tell her I'll have forgotten all about her
    Afore we cross the Line.
'N' tell her that the dollars of any other sailorman
    Is as good red gold as mine.

Is there anything as I can do aboard for you
Afore the tow-rope's taut?

I'm new to this packet and all the ways of her,
    'N' I don't know of aught;
But I knows as I'm goin' down to the seas agen
    'N' the seas are salt 'n' drear;
But I knows as all the doin' as you're man enough for
    Won't make them lager-beer.

'N' ain't there nothin' *as I can do ashore for you*
When you've got fair afloat? —

You can buy a farm with the dollars as you've done me of
'N' cash my advance-note.

Is there anythin' you'd fancy for your breakfastin'
When you're home across Mersey Bar? —

I wants a red herrin' 'n' a prairie oyster
'N' a bucket of Three Star,
'N' a gell with redder lips than Polly has got,
'N' prettier ways than Nan —

Well, so-long, Billy, 'n' a spankin' heavy pay-day tc you!

So-long, my fancy man!

A NIGHT AT DAGO TOM'S

Oh yesterday, I t'ink it was, while cruisin' down the street,
I met with Bill. — 'Hullo,' he says, 'let's give the girls a
    treat.'
We'd red bandanas round our necks 'n' our shrouds new
    rattled down,
So we filled a couple of Santy Cruz and cleared for Sailor
    Town.

We scooted south with a press of sail till we fetched to a
    caboose,
The 'Sailor's Rest,' by Dago Tom, alongside 'Paddy's
    Goose.'
Red curtains to the windies, ay, 'n' white sand to the
    floor,
And an old blind fiddler liltin' the tune of 'Lowlands no
    more.'

He played the 'Shaking of the Sheets' 'n' the couples
    did advance,
Bowing, stamping, curtsying, in the shuffling of the
    dance;
The old floor rocked and quivered, so it struck beholders
    dumb,

'N' arterwards there was sweet songs 'n' good Jamaikey
    rum.

'N' there was many a merry yarn of many a merry spree
Aboard the ships with royals set a-sailing on the sea,
Yarns of the hooker 'Spindrift,' her as had the clipper-
    bow, —
'There ain't no ships,' says Bill to me, 'like that there
    hooker now.'

When the old blind fiddler played the tune of 'Pipe the
    Watch Below,'
The skew-eyed landlord dowsed the glim and bade us
    'stamp 'n' go,'
'N' we linked it home, did Bill 'n' I, adown the scattered
    streets,
Until we fetched to Land o' Nod atween the linen sheets.

PORT OF MANY SHIPS

'It's a sunny pleasant anchorage, is Kingdom Come,
Where crews is always layin' aft for double-tots o'
    rum,
'N' there's dancin' 'n' fiddlin' of ev'ry kind o' sort,
It's a fine place for sailor-men is that there port.
      'N' I wish —
      I wish as I was there.

'The winds is never nothin' more than jest light airs,
'N' no-one gets belayin'-pinned, 'n' no-one never swears,
Yer free to loaf an' laze around, yer pipe atween yer
    lips,
Lollin' on the fo'c's'le, sonny, lookin' at the ships.
      'N' I wish —
      I wish as I was there.

'For ridin' in the anchorage the ships of all the world
Have got one anchor down 'n' all sails furled.
All the sunken hookers 'n' the crews as took 'n' died
They lays there merry, sonny, swingin' to the tide.
      'N' I wish —
      I wish as I was there.

'Drowned old wooden hookers green wi' drippin' wrack,
Ships as never fetched to port, as never came back,
Swingin' to the blushin' tide, dippin' to the swell,
'N' the crews all singin', sonny, beatin' on the bell.
     'N' I wish —
     I wish as I was there.'

CAPE HORN GOSPEL — I

'I was in a hooker once,' said Karlssen,
'And Bill, as was a seaman, died,
So we lashed him in an old tarpaulin
And tumbled him across the side;
And the fun of it was that all his gear was
Divided up among the crew
Before that blushing human error,
Our crawling little captain, knew.

'On the passage home one morning
(As certain as I prays for grace)
There was old Bill's shadder a-hauling
At the weather mizzen-topsail brace.
He was all grown green with sea-weed,
He was all lashed up and shored;
So I says to him, I says, "Why, Billy!
What's a-bringin' of you back aboard?"

'"I'm a-weary of them there mermaids,"
Says old Bill's ghost to me;
"It ain't no place for a Christian
Below there — under sea.
For it's all blown sand and shipwrecks,

And old bones eaten bare,
And them cold fishy females
With long green weeds for hair.

'"And there ain't no dances shuffled,
And no old yarns is spun,
And there ain't no stars but starfish,
And never any moon or sun.
I heard your keel a-passing
And the running rattle of the brace,"
And he says, "Stand by," says William,
"For a shift towards a better place."

'Well, he sogered about decks till sunrise,
When a rooster in the hen-coop crowed,
And as so much smoke he faded
And as so much smoke he goed;
And I've often wondered since, Jan,
How his old ghost stands to fare
Long o' them cold fishy females
With long green weeds for hair.'

CAPE HORN GOSPEL — II

Jake was a dirty Dago lad, an' he gave the skipper chin,
An' the skipper up an' took him a crack with an iron
belaying-pin
Which stiffened him out a rusty corp, as pretty as you
could wish,
An' then we shovelled him up in a sack an' dumped him
to the fish.
That was jest arter we'd got sail on her.

Josey slipped from the tops'l-yard an' bust his bloody
back
(Which comed from playing the giddy goat an' leavin'
go the jack);
We lashed his chips in clouts of sail an' ballasted him
with stones,
'The Lord hath taken away,' we says, an' we give him
to Davy Jones.
An' that was afore we were up with the Line.

Joe were chippin' a rusty plate a-squattin' upon the deck,
An' all the watch he had the sun a-singein' him on the
neck,
An' forrard he falls at last, he does, an' he lets his mallet
go,

Dead as a nail with a calenture, an' that was the end of
　　Joe.
　　　　An' that was just afore we made the Plate.

All o' the rest were sailor-men, an' it come to rain an'
　　squall,
An' then it was halliards, sheets, an 'tacks 'clue up, an'
　　let go all.'
We snugged her down an' hove her to, an' the old con-
　　trairy cuss
Started a plate, an' settled an' sank, an' that was the end
　　of us.

We slopped around on coops an' planks in the cold an'
　　in the dark,
An' Bill were drowned, an' Tom were ate by a swine of
　　a cruel shark,
An' a mail-boat reskied Harry an' I (which comed of
　　pious prayers),
Which brings me here a-kickin' my heels in the port of
　　Buenos Ayres.

I'm bound for home in the 'Oronook,' in a suit of looted
　　duds,
A D.B.S. a-earnin' a stake by helpin' peelin' spuds,
An' if ever I fetch to Prince's Stage an' sets my feet
　　ashore,
You bet your hide that there I stay, an' follers the sea
　　no more.

MOTHER CAREY

(AS TOLD ME BY THE BO'SUN)

MOTHER CAREY? She's the mother o' the witches
  'N' all *them* sort o' rips;
She's a fine gell to look at, but the hitch is,
  She's a sight too fond of ships.
She lives upon a iceberg to the norred,
  'N' her man he's Davy Jones,
'N' she combs the weeds upon her forred
  With pore drowned sailors' bones.

She's the mother o' the wrecks, 'n' the mother
  Of all big winds as blows;
She's up to some deviltry or other
  When it storms, or sleets, or snows.
The noise of the wind's her screamin',
  'I'm arter a plump, young, fine,
Brass-buttoned, beefy-ribbed young seam'n
  So as me 'n' my mate kin dine.'

She's a hungry old rip 'n' a cruel
  For sailor-men like we,
She's give a many mariners the gruel
  'N' a long sleep under sea.

She's the blood o' many a crew upon her
  'N' the bones of many a wreck,
'N' she's barnacles a-growin' on her
  'N' shark's teeth round her neck.

I ain't never had no schoolin'
  Nor read no books like you,
But I knows 't ain't healthy to be foolin'
  With that there gristly two.
You're young, you thinks, 'n' you're lairy,
  But if you're to make old bones,
Steer clear, I says, o' Mother Carey,
  'N' that there Davy Jones.

EVENING — REGATTA DAY

Your nose is a red jelly, your mouth's a toothless wreck,
And I'm atop of you, banging your head upon the dirty
deck;
And both your eyes are bunged and blind like those of a
mewling pup,
For you're the juggins who caught the crab and lost the
ship the Cup.

He caught a crab in the spurt home, this blushing cherub did,
And the 'Craigie's' whaler slipped ahead like a cart-wheel
on the skid,
And beat us fair by a boat's nose though we sweated fit
to start her,
So we are playing at Nero now, and *he's* the Christian
martyr.

And Stroke is lashing a bunch of keys to the buckle-end
a belt,
And we're going to lay you over a chest and baste you till
you melt.
The 'Craigie' boys are beating the bell and cheering down
the tier,
D'ye hear, you Port Mahone baboon, I ask you, do you
hear?

A VALEDICTION

We're bound for blue water where the great winds blow,
It's time to get the tacks aboard, time for us to go;
The crowd's at the capstan and the tune's in the shout,
'A long pull, a strong pull, *and warp the hooker out.*'

The bow-wash is eddying, spreading from the bows,
Aloft and loose the topsails and some one give a rouse;
A salt Atlantic chanty shall be music to the dead,
'A long pull, a strong pull, *and the yard to the masthead.*'

Green and merry run the seas, the wind comes cold,
Salt and strong and pleasant, and worth a mint of gold;
And she's staggering, swooping, as she feels her feet,
'A long pull, a strong pull, *and aft the main-sheet.*'

Shrilly squeal the running sheaves, the weather-gear
      strains,
Such a clatter of chain-sheets, the devil's in the chains;
Over us the bright stars, under us the drowned,
'A long pull, a strong pull, *and we're outward bound.*'

Yonder, round and ruddy, is the mellow old moon,
The red-funnelled tug has gone, and now, sonny, soon
We'll be clear of the Channel, so watch how you steer,
'Ease her when she pitches, *and so-long, my dear.*'

E   49

The bow-wash is eddying, spreading from the bows,
Aloft and loose the topsails and some one give a rouse;
A salt Atlantic chanty shall be music to the dead,
'A long pull, a strong pull, *and the yard to the masthead.*'

A PIER–HEAD CHORUS

OH I'll be chewing salted horse and biting flinty bread,
And dancing with the stars to watch, upon the fo'c's'le head,
Hearkening to the bow-wash and the welter of the tread
  Of a thousand tons of clipper running free.

For the tug has got the tow-rope and will take us to the
    Downs,
Her paddles churn the river-wrack to muddy greens and
    browns,
And I have given river-wrack and all the filth of towns
  For the rolling, combing cresters of the sea.

We'll sheet the mizzen-royals home and shimmer down
    the Bay,
The sea-line blue with billows, the land-line blurred and
    grey;
The bow-wash will be piling high and thrashing into spray,
  As the hooker's fore-foot tramples down the swell.

She'll log a giddy seventeen and rattle out the reel,
The weight of all the run-out line will be a thing to feel,
As the bacca-quidding shell-back shambles aft to take
    the wheel,
  And the sea-sick little middy strikes the bell.

51

Chas. Pears.

She'll log a giddy seventeen and rattle out the reel,
The weight of all the run-out line will be a thing to feel,
As the bacca-quidding shell-back shambles aft to take the wheel,
  And the sea-sick little middy strikes the bell.

THE GOLDEN CITY OF ST. MARY

OUT beyond the sunset, could I but find the way,
Is a sleepy blue laguna which widens to a bay,
And there's the Blessed City — so the sailors say —
　The Golden City of St. Mary.

It's built of fair marble — white — without a stain,
And in the cool twilight when the sea-winds wane
The bells chime faintly, like a soft, warm rain,
　In the Golden City of St. Mary.

Among the green palm-trees where the fire-flies shine,
Are the white tavern tables where the gallants dine,
Singing slow Spanish songs like old mulled wine,
　In the Golden City of St. Mary.

Oh I'll be shipping sunset-wards and westward-ho
Through the green toppling combers a-shattering into
　snow,
Till I come to quiet moorings and a watch below,
　In the Golden City of St. Mary.

TRADE WINDS

In the harbour, in the island, in the Spanish Seas,
Are the tiny white houses and the orange-trees,
And day-long, night long, the cool and pleasant breeze
  Of the steady Trade Winds blowing.

There is the red wine, the nutty Spanish ale,
The shuffle of the dancers, the old salt's tale,
The squeaking fiddle, and the soughing in the sail
  Of the steady Trade Winds blowing.

And o' nights there's fire-flies and the yellow moon,
And in the ghostly palm-trees the sleepy tune
Of the quiet voice calling me, the long low croon
Of the steady Trade Winds blowing.

SEA-FEVER

I must go down to the seas again, to the lonely sea and the
    sky,
And all I ask is a tall ship and a star to steer her by,
And the wheel's kick and the wind's song and the white
    sail's shaking,
And a grey mist on the sea's face and a grey dawn breaking.

I must go down to the seas again, for the call of the running
    tide
Is a wild call and a clear call that may not be denied;
And all I ask is a windy day with the white clouds flying,
And the flung spray and the blown spume, and the sea-
    gulls crying.

I must go down to the seas again to the vagrant gypsy life,
To the gull's way and the whale's way where the wind's
    like a whetted knife;
And all I ask is a merry yarn from a laughing fellow-rover,
And quiet sleep and a sweet dream when the long trick's
    over.

A WANDERER'S SONG

A WIND's in the heart of me, a fire's in my heels,
I am tired of brick and stone and rumbling wagon-wheels:
I hunger for the sea's edge, the limits of the land,
Where the wild old Atlantic is shouting on the sand.

Oh I'll be going, leaving the noises of the street,
To where a lifting foresail-foot is yanking at the sheet;
To a windy, tossing anchorage where yawls and ketchei
    ride,
Oh I'll be going, going, until I meet the tide.

And first I'll hear the sea-wind, the mewing of the gulls,
The clucking, sucking of the sea about the rusty hulls,
The songs at the capstan in the hooker warping out,
And then the heart of me'll know I'm there or there-
    about.

Oh I am tired of brick and stone, the heart of me is sick
For windy green, unquiet sea, the realm of Moby Dick
And I'll be going, going, from the roaring of the wheels
For a wind's in the heart of me, a fire's in my heels.

CARDIGAN BAY

CLEAN, green, windy billows notching out the sky,
Grey clouds tattered into rags, sea-winds blowing high,
And the ships under topsails, beating, thrashing by,
   And the mewing of the herring gulls.

Dancing, flashing green seas shaking white locks,
Boiling in blind eddies over hidden rocks,
And the wind in the rigging, the creaking of the blocks,
   And the straining of the timber hulls.

Delicate, cool sea-weeds, green and amber-brown,
In beds where shaken sunlight slowly filters down
On many a drowned seventy-four, many a sunken town
   And the whitening of the dead men's skulls.

CHRISTMAS EVE AT SEA

A WIND is rustling 'south and soft,'
  Cooing a quiet country tune,
The calm sea sighs, and far aloft
  The sails are ghostly in the moon.

Unquiet ripples lisp and purr,
  A block there pipes and chirps i' the sheave,
The wheel-ropes jar, the reef-points stir
  Faintly — and it is Christmas Eve.

The hushed sea seems to hold her breath,
  And o'er the giddy, swaying spars,
Silent and excellent as Death,
  The dim blue skies are bright with stars

Dear God — they shone in Palestine
  Like this, and yon pale moon serene
Looked down among the lowing kine
  On Mary and the Nazarene.

The angels called from deep to deep,
  The burning heavens felt the thrill,
Startling the flocks of silly sheep
  And lonely shepherds on the hill.

To-night beneath the dripping bows
  Where flashing bubbles burst and throng,
The bow-wash murmurs and sighs and soughs
  A message from the angel's song.

The moon goes nodding down the west,
  The drowsy helmsman strikes the bell;
Rex Judæorum natus est,
  I charge you, brothers, sing *Nowell,*
  Nowell,
Rex Judæorum natus est.

A BALLAD OF CAPE ST. VINCENT

Now, Bill, ain't it prime to be a-sailin',
  Slippin' easy, splashin' up the sea,
Dossin' snug aneath the weather-railin',
  Quiddin' bonded Jacky out a-lee?
English sea astern us and afore us,
  Reaching out three thousand miles ahead,
God's own stars a-risin' solemn o'er us,
  And — yonder's Cape St. Vincent and the Dead.

There they lie, Bill, man and mate together,
  Dreamin' out the dog-watch down below,
Anchored in the Port of Pleasant Weather,
  Waiting for the Bo'sun's call to blow.
Over them the tide goes lappin', swayin',
  Under them's the wide bay's muddy bed,
And it's pleasant dreams — to them — to hear us sayin',
  Yonder's Cape St. Vincent and the Dead.

Hear that P. and O. boat's engines dronin',
  Beating out of time and out of tune,
Ripping past with every plate a-groanin',
  Spitting smoke and cinders at the moon?
Ports a-lit like little stars a-settin',
  See 'em glintin' yaller, green, and red,

Loggin' twenty knots, Dill,   but forgettin',
   Yonder's Cape St. Vincent and the Dead.

They're 'discharged' now, Billy, 'left the service,'
   Rough an' bitter was the watch they stood,
Drake an' Blake, an' Collingwood an' Jervis,
   Nelson, Rodney, Hawke, an' Howe an' Hood.
They'd a hard time, haulin' an' directin',
   There's the flag they left us, Billy — tread
Straight an' keep it flyin' — recollectin',
   Yonder's Cape St. Vincent and the Dead.

THE TARRY BUCCANEER

I'M going to be a pirate with a bright brass pivot-gun,
And an island in the Spanish Main beyond the setting
sun,
And a silver flagon full of red wine to drink when work is
done,
Like a fine old salt-sea scavenger, like a tarry Buc-
caneer.

With a sandy creek to careen in, and a pig-tailed Spanish
mate,
And under my main-hatches a sparkling merry freight
Of doubloons and double moidores and pieces of eight,
Like a fine old salt-sea scavenger, like a tarry Buc-
caneer.

With a taste for Spanish wine-shops and for spending
my doubloons,
And a crew of swart mulattoes and black-eyed octo-
roons,
And a thoughtful way with mutineers of making them
maroons,
Like a fine old salt-sea scavenger, like a tarry Buc-
caneer.

With a sash of crimson velvet and a diamond-hilted sword,
And a silver whistle about my neck secured to a golden
cord,
And a habit of taking captives and walking them along
a board,
Like a fine old salt-sea scavenger, like a tarry Buc-
caneer.

With a spy-glass tucked beneath my arm and a cocked
hat cocked askew,
And a long low rakish schooner a-cutting of the waves
in two,
And a flag of skull and cross-bones the wickedest that
ever flew,
Like a fine old salt-sea scavenger, like a tarry Buc-
caneer.

A BALLAD OF JOHN SILVER

WE were schooner-rigged and rakish, with a long and
lissome hull,
And we flew the pretty colours of the cross-bones and
the skull;
We'd a big black Jolly Roger flapping grimly at the
fore,
And we sailed the Spanish Water in the happy days of
yore.

We'd a long brass gun amidships, like a well-conducted
ship,
We had each a brace of pistols and a cutlass at the hip;
It's a point which tells against us, and a fact to be deplored,
But we chased the goodly merchant-men and laid their
ships aboard.

Then the dead men fouled the scuppers and the wounded
filled the chains,
And the paint-work all was spatter-dashed with other
people's brains,
She was boarded, she was looted, she was scuttled till
she sank,
And the pale survivors left us by the medium of the
plank.

O! then it was (while standing by the taffrail on the
    poop)
We could hear the drowning folk lament the absent
    chicken-coop;
Then, having washed the blood away, we'd little else
    to do
Than to dance a quiet hornpipe as the old salts taught
    us to.

O! the fiddle on the fo'c's'le, and the slapping naked
    soles,
And the genial 'Down the middle, Jake, and curtsey
    when she rolls!'
With the silver seas around us and the pale moon over-
    head,
And the look-out not a-looking and his pipe-bowl glowing
    red.

Ah! the pig-tailed, quidding pirates and the pretty pranks
    we played,
All have since been put a stop-to by the naughty Board
    of Trade;
The schooners and the merry crews are laid away to rest,
A little south the sunset in the Islands of the Blest.

LYRICS FROM 'THE BUCCANEER'

I

WE are far from sight of the harbour lights,
  Of the sea-ports whence we came,
But the old sea calls and the cold wind bites,
  And our hearts are turned to flame.

And merry and rich is the goodly gear
  We'll win upon the tossing sea,
A silken gown for my dainty dear,
  And a gold doubloon for me.

It's the old old road and the old old quest
  Of the cut-throat sons of Cain,
South by west and a quarter west,
  And hey for the Spanish Main.

II

THERE'S a sea-way somewhere where all day long
  Is the hushed susurrus of the sea,
The mewing of the skuas, and the sailor's song,
  And the wind's cry calling me.

There's a haven somewhere where the quiet of the bay
  Is troubled with the shifting tide,

Where the gulls are flying, crying in the bright white
    spray,
  And the tan-sailed schooners ride.

III

THE toppling rollers at the harbour mouth
  Are spattering the bows with foam,
And the anchor's catted, and she's heading for the south
  With her topsails sheeted home.

And a merry measure is the dance she'll tread
  (To the clanking of the staysail's hanks)
When the guns are growling and the blood runs red,
  And the prisoners are walking of the planks.

D'AVALOS' PRAYER

WHEN the last sea is sailed and the last shallow charted,
  When the last field is reaped and the last harvest
  stored,
When the last fire is out and the last guest departed,
  Grant the last prayer that I shall pray, Be good to
  me, O Lord!

And let me pass in a night at sea, a night of storm and
  thunder,
  In the loud crying of the wind through sail and rope
  and spar;
Send me a ninth great peaceful wave to drown and roll
  me under
  To the cold tunny-fishes' home where the drowned
  galleons are.

And in the dim green quiet place far out of sight and
  hearing,
  Grant I may hear at whiles the wash and thresh of the
  sea-foam
About the fine keen bows of the stately clippers steering
  Towards the lone northern star and the fair ports of
  home.

SEA PICTURES

FROM *PHILIP THE KING*

MESSENGER

WE were to ship the troops in Calais Road;
They lay encamped, prepared to go aboard.
To windward still the English fleet abode —
Still as in port when peace has been restored.

The wind and sea were fair,
We lay at anchor there;
The stars burned in the air,
The men were sleeping,
When in the midnight dark
Our watchman saw a spark
Suddenly light a bark
With long flames leaping.

Then, as they stood amazed,
Others and others blazed;
Then terror set them crazed,
They ran down screaming:
"Fire-ships are coming! Wake!
Cast loose, for Jesus' sake!
Eight fire-ships come from Drake —
Look at their gleaming!"

Roused in the dark from bed,
We saw the fire show red,
And instant panic spread
Through troops and sailors;
They swarmed on deck unclad,
They did what terror bade,
King, they were like the mad
Escaped from jailers.

Some prayed for mercy, some
Rang bells or beat the drum,
As though despair had come
At hell's contriving;
Captains with terror pale
Screamed through the dark their hail,
"Cut cable, loose the sail,
And set all driving!"

Heading all ways at once,
Grinding each other's guns,
Our blundering galleons
Athwart-hawse galleys,
Timbers and plankings cleft,
And half our tackling reft,
Your grand Armada left
The roads of Calais.

Weary and overwrought
We strove to make all taut;
But when the morning brought

The dawn to light us,
Drake, with the weather gage,
Made signal to engage,
And, like a pard in rage,
Bore down to fight us.

Nobly the English line
Trampled the bubbled brine;
We heard the gun-trucks whine
To the taut laniard.
Onwards we saw them forge,
White billowing at the gorge.
"On, on!" they cried, "St. George!
Down with the Spaniard!"

From their van squadron broke
A withering battle-stroke,
Tearing our plankèd oak
By straiks asunder,
Blasting the wood like rot
With such a hail of shot,
So constant and so hot
It beat us under.

The English would not close;
They fought us as they chose,
Dealing us deadly blows
For seven hours.

Lords of our chiefest rank
The bitter billow drank,
For there the English sank
Three ships of ours.

*   *   *   *   *   *   *

Then the wind forced us northward from the fight;
We could not ship the army nor return;
We held the sea in trouble through the night,
Watching the English signals blink and burn.
The English in a dim cloud kept astern;
All night they signalled, while our shattered ships
Huddled like beasts beneath the drovers' whips.

*   *   *   *   *   *   *

At dawn the same wind held; we could not strive.
The English drove us north as herdsmen drive.

*   *   *   *   *   *   *

Under our tattered flags,
With rigging cut to rags,
Our ships like stricken stags
Were heaped and hounded.
Caught by the unknown tide,
With neither chart nor guide,
We fouled the Holland side,
Where four more grounded.

Our water-casks were burst,
The horses died of thirst,
The wounded raved and curst,
Uncared, untended.
All night we heard the crying
Of lonely shipmates dying;
We had to leave them lying.
So the fight ended.

Philip

God gives His victory as He wills.   But this
Was not complete destruction.   What thing worse
Came to destroy you?

Messenger

                    An avenging curse,
Due for old sins, destroyed us.

Philip

                       Tell the tale.

Messenger

O King, when morning dawned it blew a gale,
But still the English followed, and we fled
Till breakers made the dirty waters pale.
We saw the Zealand sandbanks right ahead,
Blind in a whirling spray that gave us dread;
For we were blown there, and the water shoaled.
The crying of the leadsmen at the lead,
Calling the soundings, were our deathbells tolled.

We drifted down to death upon the sands —
The English drew away to watch us drown;
We saw the bitter breakers with grey hands
Tear the dead body of the sandbank brown.
We could do nothing, so we drifted down
Singing the psalms for death — we who had been
Lords of the sea and knights of great renown,
Doomed to be strangled by a death unclean.

PHILIP

So there the ships were wrecked?

MESSENGER

                    Time had not struck.
O King, we learned how blessed mercy saves:
Even as our forefoot grounded on the muck,
Tripping us up to drown us in the waves,
A sudden windshift snatched us from our graves
And drove us north; and now another woe,
Tempest unending, beat our ships to staves —
A never-dying gale with frost and snow.

Now our hearts failed, for food and water failed;
The men fell sick by troops, the wounded died.
They washed about the wet decks as we sailed
For want of strength to lift them overside.
Desolate seas we sailed, so grim, so wide,
That ship by ship our comrades disappeared.
With neither sun nor star to be a guide,
Like spirits of the wretched dead we steered.

Till, having beaten through the Pentland Pass,
We saw the Irish surf, with mists of spray
Blowing far inland, blasting trees and grass,
And gave God thanks, for we espied a bay
Safe, with bright water running down the clay —
A running brook where we could drink and drink.
But drawing near, our ships were cast away,
Bilged on the rocks; we saw our comrades sink . . .

Or worse: for those the breakers cast ashore
The Irish killed and stripped; their bodies white
Lay naked to the wolves — yea, sixty score —
All down the windy beach, a piteous sight.
The savage Irish watched by bonfire light
Lest more should come ashore; we heard them there
Screaming the bloody news of their delight.
Then we abandoned hope and new despair.

And now the fleet is sunken in the sea,
And all the seamen, all the might of Spain,
Are dead, O King, and out of misery,
Never to drag at frozen ropes again —
Never to know defeat, nor feel the pain
Of watching dear companions sink and die.
Death's everlasting armistice to the brain
Gives their poor griefs quietus; let them lie.

I, like a ghost returning from the grave,
Come from a stricken ship to tell the news
Of Spanish honour which we could not save,

Nor win again, nor even die to lose;
And since God's hidden wisdom loves to bruise
Those whom He loves, we, trembling in despair,
Will watch our griefs to see God's finger there,
And make His will our solace and excuse.

Defeat is bitter and the truth is hard —
Spain is defeated, England has prevailed;
This is the banner which I could not guard,
And this the consecrated sword which failed.
Do with your dying Captain as you will.

FROM *DAUBER*

Four bells were struck, the watch was called on deck,
All work aboard was over for the hour,
And some men sang and others played at check,
Or mended clothes or watched the sunset glower.
The bursting west was like an opening flower,
And one man watched it till the light was dim,
But no one went across to talk to him.

He was the painter in that swift ship's crew,
Lampman and painter — tall, a slight-built man,
Young for his years, and not yet twenty-two;
Sickly, and not yet brown with the sea's tan.
Bullied and damned at since the voyage began,
"Being neither man nor seaman by his tally,"
He bunked with the idlers just abaft the galley.

His work began at five; he worked all day,
Keeping no watch and having all night in.
His work was what the mate might care to say;
He mixed red lead in many a bouilli tin;
His dungarees were smeared with paraffin.
"Go drown himself" his round-house mates advised
    him,
And all hands called him "Dauber" and despised him.

79

Si, the apprentice, stood beside the spar,
Stripped to the waist, a basin at his side,
Slushing his hands to get away the tar,
And then he washed himself and rinsed and dried;
Towelling his face, hair-towzelled, eager eyed,
He crossed the spar to Dauber, and there stood
Watching the gold of heaven turn to blood.

They stood there by the rail while the swift ship
Tore on out of the tropics, straining her sheets,
Whitening her trackway to a milky strip,
Dim with green bubbles and twisted water meets,
Her clacking tackle tugged at pins and cleats,
Her great sails bellied stiff, her great masts leaned:
They watched how the seas struck and burst and greened.

Si talked with Dauber, standing by the side.
"Why did you come to sea, painter?" he said.
"I want to be a painter," he replied,
"And know the sea and ships from A to Z,
And paint great ships at sea before I'm dead;
Ships under skysails running down the Trade —
Ships and the sea; there's nothing finer made.

"But there's so much to learn, with sails and ropes,
And how the sails look, full or being furled,
And how the lights change in the troughs and slopes
And the sea's colours up and down the world,
And how a storm looks when the sprays are hurled

High as the yard (they say) I want to see;
There's none ashore can teach such things to me.

"And then the men and rigging, and the way
Ships move, running or beating, and the poise
At the roll's end, the checking in the sway —
I want to paint them perfect, short of the noise;
And then the life, the half-decks full of boys,
The fo'c'sles with the men there, dripping wet:
I know the subjects that I want to get.

"It's not been done, the sea, not yet been done,
From the inside, by one who really knows;
I'd give up all if I could be the one,
But art comes dear the way the money goes.
So I have come to sea, and I suppose
Three years will teach me all I want to learn
And make enough to keep me till I earn."

Even as he spoke his busy pencil moved,
Drawing the leap of water off the side
Where the great clipper trampled iron-hooved,
Making the blue hills of the sea divide,
Shearing a glittering scatter in her stride,
And leaping on full tilt with all sails drawing,
Proud as a war-horse, snuffing battle, pawing.

"I cannot get it yet — not yet," he said;
"That leap and light, and sudden change to green,

And all the glittering from the sunset's red,
And the milky colours where the bursts have been,
And then the clipper striding like a queen
Over it all, all beauty to the crown.
I see it all, I cannot put it down.

"It's hard not to be able.   There, look there!
I cannot get the movement nor the light;
Sometimes it almost makes a man despair
To try and try and never get it right.
Oh, if I could — oh, if I only might,
I wouldn't mind what hells I'd have to pass,
Not if the whole world called me fool and ass."

Down sank the crimson sun into the sea,
The wind cut chill at once, the west grew dun.
"Out sidelights!" called the mate.   "Hi, where is he?"
The Boatswain called, "Out sidelights, damn you!
    Run!"
"He's always late or lazing," murmured one —
"The Dauber, with his sketching."   Soon the tints
Of red and green passed on dark water-glints.

Darker it grew, still darker, and the stars
Burned golden, and the fiery fishes came.
The wire-note loudened from the straining spars;
The sheet-blocks clacked together always the same;
The rushing fishes streaked the seas with flame,
Racing the one speed noble as their own:
What unknown joy was in those fish unknown!

Just by the round house door, as it grew dark,
The Boatswain caught the Dauber with, "Now, you;
Till now I've spared you, damn you! now you hark:
I've just had hell for what you didn't do;
I'll have you broke and sent among the crew
If you get me more trouble by a particle.
Don't you forget, you daubing, useless article!

"You thing, you twice-laid thing from Port Mahon!"
Then came the Cook's "Is that the Dauber there?
Why don't you leave them stinking paints alone?
They stink the house out, poisoning all the air.
Just take them out." "Where to?" "I don't care
      where.
I won't have stinking paint here." From their plates:
"That's right; wet paint breeds fever," growled his mates.

He took his still wet drawings from the berth
And climbed the ladder to the deck-house top;
Beneath, the noisy half-deck rang with mirth,
For two ship's boys were putting on the strop:
One, clambering up to let the skylight drop,
Saw him bend down beneath a boat and lay
His drawings there, till all were hid away,

And stand there silent, leaning on the boat,
Watching the constellations rise and burn,
Until the beauty took him by the throat,
So stately is their glittering overturn;
Armies of marching eyes, armies that yearn

With banners rising and falling, and passing by
Over the empty silence of the sky.

The Dauber sighed there looking at the sails,
Wind-steadied arches leaning on the night,
The high trucks traced on heaven and left no trails;
The moonlight made the topsails almost white,
The passing sidelight seemed to drip green light.
And on the clipper rushed with fire-bright bows;
He sighed, "I'll never do't," and left the house.

"Now," said the reefer, "up! Come, Sam; come, Si,
Dauber's been hiding something." Up they slid,
Treading on naked tiptoe stealthily
To grope for treasure at the long-boat skid.
"Drawings!" said Sam. "Is this what Dauber hid?
Lord! I expected pudding, not this rot.
Still, come, we'll have some fun with what we've got."

They smeared the paint with turpentine until
They could remove with mess-clouts every trace
Of quick perception caught by patient skill,
And lines that had brought blood into his face.
They wiped the pigments off, and did erase,
With knives, all sticking clots. When they had done,
Under the boat they laid them every one.

All he had drawn since first he came to sea,
His six weeks' leisure fruits, they laid them there.

They chuckled then to think how mad he'd be
Finding his paintings vanished into air.
Eight bells were struck, and feet from everywhere
Went shuffling aft to muster in the dark;
The mate's pipe glowed above, a dim red spark.

Names in the darkness passed and voices cried;
The red spark glowed and died, the faces seemed
As things remembered when a brain has died,
To all but high intenseness deeply dreamed.
Like hissing spears the fishes' fire streamed,
And on the clipper rushed with tossing mast,
A bath of flame broke round her as she passed.

The watch was set, the night came, and the men
Hid from the moon in shadowed nooks to sleep,
Bunched like the dead; still, like the dead, as when
Plague in a city leaves none even to weep.
The ship's track brightened to a mile-broad sweep;
The mate there felt her pulse, and eyed the spars:
South-west by south she staggered under the stars.

Down in his bunk the Dauber lay awake
Thinking of his unfitness for the sea.
Each failure, each derision, each mistake,
There in the life not made for such as he;
A morning grim with trouble sure to be,
A noon of pain from failure, and a night
Bitter with men's contemning and despite.

This in the first beginning, the green leaf,
Still in the Trades before bad weather fell;
What harvest would he reap of hate and grief
When the loud Horn made every life a hell?
When the sick ship lay over, clanging her bell,
And no time came for painting or for drawing,
But all hands fought, and icy death came clawing?

Hell, he expected, — hell.   His eyes grew blind;
The snoring from his messmates droned and snuffled,
And then a gush of pity calmed his mind.
The cruel torment of his thought was muffled,
Without, on deck, an old, old seaman shuffled,
Humming his song, and through the open door
A moonbeam moved and thrust along the floor.

The green bunk curtains moved, the brass rings clicked.
The Cook cursed in his sleep, turning and turning,
The moonbeams' moving finger touched and picked,
And all the stars in all the sky were burning.
"This is the art I've come for, and am learning,
The sea and ships and men and travelling things.
It is most proud, whatever pain it brings."

He leaned upon his arm and watched the light
Sliding and fading to the steady roll;
This he would some day paint, the ship at night,
And sleeping seamen tired to the soul;
The space below the bunks as black as coal,

Gleams upon chests, upon the unlit lamp,
The ranging door hook, and the locker clamp.

This he would paint, and that, and all these scenes,
And proud ships carrying on, and men their minds,
And blues of rollers toppling into greens,
And shattering into white that bursts and blinds,
And scattering ships running erect like hinds,
And men in oilskins beating down a sail
High on the yellow yard, in snow, in hail.

With faces ducked down from the slanting drive
Of half-thawed hail mixed with half-frozen spray,
The roaring canvas like a thing alive,
Shaking the mast, knocking their hands away,
The foot-ropes jerking to the tug and sway,
The savage eyes salt-reddened at the rims,
And icicles on the south-wester brims.

And sunnier scenes would grow under his brush,
The tropic dawn with all things dropping dew,
The darkness and the wonder and the hush,
The insensate grey before the marvel grew;
Then the veil lifted from the trembling blue,
The walls of sky burst in, the flower, the rose,
All the expanse of heaven a mind that glows.

He turned out of his bunk; the Cook still tossed,
One of the other two spoke in his sleep.

A cockroach scuttled where the moonbeam crossed;
Outside there was the ship, the night, the deep.
"It is worth while," the youth said; "I will keep
To my resolve, I'll learn to paint all this.
My Lord, my God, how beautiful it is!"

Outside was the ship's rush to the wind's hurry,
A resonant wire-hum from every rope,
The broadening bow-wash in a fiery flurry,
The leaning masts in their majestic slope,
And all things strange with moonlight: filled with hope
By all that beauty going as man bade,
He turned and slept in peace.   Eight bells were made.

That night the snow fell between six and seven,
A little feathery fall so light, so dry —
An aimless dust out of a confused heaven,
Upon an air no steadier than a sigh;
The powder dusted down and wandered by
So purposeless, so many, and so cold,
Then died, and the wind ceased and the ship rolled.

Rolled till she clanged — rolled till the brain was tired,
Marking the acme of the heaves, the pause
While the sea-beauty rested and respired,
Drinking great draughts of roller at her hawse.
Flutters of snow came aimless upon flaws.
"Lock up your paints," the Mate said, speaking light:
"This is the Horn; you'll join my watch to-night!"

All through the windless night the clipper rolled
In a great swell with oily gradual heaves
Which rolled her down until her time-bells tolled,
Clang, and the weltering water moaned like beeves.
The thundering rattle of slatting shook the sheaves,
Startles of water made the swing ports gush,
The sea was moaning and sighing and saying "Hush!"

It was all black and starless.   Peering down
Into the water, trying to pierce the gloom,
One saw a dim, smooth, oily glitter of brown
Heaving and dying away and leaving room
For yet another.   Like the march of doom
Came those great powers of marching silences;
Then fog came down, dead-cold, and hid the seas.

They set the Dauber to the foghorn.   There
He stood upon the poop, making to sound
Out of the pump the sailor's nasal blare,
Listening lest ice should make the note resound.
She bayed there like a solitary hound
Lost in a covert; all the watch she bayed.
The fog, come closelier down, no answer made.

Denser it grew, until the ship was lost.
The elemental hid her; she was merged
In mufflings of dark death, like a man's ghost,
New to the change of death, yet thither urged.
Then from the hidden waters something surged —

Mournful, despairing, great, greater than speech,
A noise like one slow wave on a still beach.

Mournful, and then again mournful, and still
Out of the night that mighty voice arose;
The Dauber at his foghorn felt the thrill.
Who rode that desolate sea? What forms were those?
Mournful, from things defeated, in the throes
Of memory of some conquered hunting-ground,
Out of the night of death arose the sound.

"Whales!" said the Mate. They stayed there all night
    long
Answering the horn. Out of the night they spoke,
Defeated creatures who had suffered wrong,
But were still noble underneath the stroke.
They filled the darkness when the Dauber woke;
The men came peering to the rail to hear,
And the sea sighed, and the fog rose up sheer.

A wall of nothing at the world's last edge,
Where no life came except defeated life.
The Dauber felt shut in within a hedge,
Behind which form was hidden and thought was rife,
And that a blinding flash, a thrust, a knife
Would sweep the hedge away and make all plain,
Brilliant beyond all words, blinding the brain.

So the night passed, but then no morning broke—
Only a something showed that night was dead.

A sea-bird, cackling like a devil, spoke,
And the fog drew away and hung like lead.
Like mighty cliffs it shaped, sullen and red;
Like glowering gods at watch it did appear,
And sometimes drew away, and then drew near.

Like islands, and like chasms, and like hell,
But always mighty and red, gloomy and ruddy,
Shutting the visible sea in like a well;
Slow heaving in vast ripples, blank and muddy,
Where the sun should have risen it streaked bloody.
The day was still-born; all the sea-fowl scattering
Splashed the still water, mewing, hovering, clattering.

Then Polar snow came down little and light,
Till all the sky was hidden by the small,
Most multitudinous drift of dirty white
Tumbling and wavering down and covering all —
Covering the sky, the sea, the clipper tall,
Furring the ropes with white, casing the mast,
Coming on no known air, but blowing past.

And all the air seemed full of gradual moan,
As though in those cloud-chasms the horns were blowing
The mort for gods cast out and overthrown,
Or for the eyeless sun plucked out and going.
Slow the low gradual moan came in the snowing;
The Dauber felt the prelude had begun.
The snowstorm fluttered by; he saw the sun

Show and pass by, gleam from one towering prison
Into another, vaster and more grim,
Which in dull crags of darkness had arisen
To muffle-to a final door on him.
The gods upon the dull crags lowered dim,
The pigeons chattered, quarrelling in the track.
In the south-west the dimness dulled to black.

Then came the cry of "Call all hands on deck!"
The Dauber knew its meaning; it was come:
Cape Horn, that tramples beauty into wreck,
And crumples steel and smites the strong man dumb.
Down clattered flying kites and staysails: some
Sang out in quick, high calls: the fair-leads skirled
And from the south-west came the end of the world.

"Caught in her ball-dress," said the Bosun, hauling;
"Lee-ay, lee-ay!" quick, high, came the men's call;
It was all wallop of sails and startled calling.
"Let fly!" "Let go!" "Clew up!" and "Let go
        all!"
"Now up and make them fast!"   "Here, give us a haul!"
"Now up and stow them! Quick! By God! we're done!"
The blackness crunched all memory of the sun.

"Up!" said the Mate. "Mizzen top-gallants. Hurry!"
The Dauber ran, the others ran, the sails
Slatted and shook; out of the black a flurry
Whirled in fine lines, tattering the edge to trails.

Painting and art and England were old tales
Told in some other life to that pale man,
Who struggled with white fear and gulped and ran.

He struck a ringbolt in his haste and fell —
Rose, sick with pain, half-lamed in his left knee;
He reached the shrouds where clambering men pell-mell
Hustled each other up and cursed him; he
Hurried aloft with them: then from the sea
Came a cold, sudden breath that made the hair
Stiff on the neck, as though Death whispered there.

A man below him punched him in the side.
"Get up, you Dauber, or let me get past."
He saw the belly of the skysail skied,
Gulped, and clutched tight, and tried to go more fast.
Sometimes he missed his ratline and was grassed,
Scraped his shin raw against the rigid line.
The clamberers reached the futtock-shrouds' incline.

Cursing they came; one, kicking out behind,
Kicked Dauber in the mouth, and one below
Punched at his calves; the futtock-shrouds inclined.
It was a perilous path for one to go.
"Up, Dauber, up!" A curse followed a blow.
He reached the top and gasped, then on, then on.
And one voice yelled "Let go!" and one "All gone!"

Fierce clamberers, some in oilskins, some in rags,
Hustling and hurrying up, up the steep stairs.

Before the windless sails were blown to flags,
And whirled like dirty birds athwart great airs,
Ten men in all, to get this mast of theirs
Snugged to the gale in time.   "Up! Damn you, run!"
The mizzen topmast head was safely won.

"Lay out!" the Bosun yelled.   The Dauber laid
Out on the yard, gripping the yard, and feeling
Sick at the mighty space of air displayed
Below his feet, where mewing birds were wheeling.
A giddy fear was on him; he was reeling.
He bit his lip half through, clutching the jack.
A cold sweat glued the shirt upon his back.

The yard was shaking, for a brace was loose.
He felt that he would fall; he clutched, he bent,
Clammy with natural terror to the shoes
While idiotic promptings came and went.
Snow fluttered on a wind-flaw and was spent;
He saw the water darken.   Someone yelled,
"Frap it; don't stay to furl!   Hold on!"   He held.

Darkness came down — half darkness — in a whirl;
The sky went out, the waters disappeared.
He felt a shocking pressure of blowing hurl
The ship upon her side.   The darkness speared
At her with wind; she staggered, she careered,
Then down she lay.   The Dauber felt her go;
He saw his yard tilt downwards.   Then the snow

Whirled all about — dense, multitudinous, cold —
Mixed with the wind's one devilish thrust and shriek,
Which whiffled out men's tears, deafened, took hold,
Flattening the flying drift against the cheek.
The yards buckled and bent, man could not speak.
The ship lay on her broadside; the wind's sound
Had devilish malice at having got her downed.

* * * * * * *

How long the gale had blown he could not tell,
Only the world had changed, his life had died.
A moment now was everlasting hell.
Nature an onslaught from the weather side,
A withering rush of death, a frost that cried,
Shrieked, till he withered at the heart; a hail
Plastered his oilskins with an icy mail.

"Cut!" yelled his mate. He looked — the sail was
    gone,
Blown into rags in the first furious squall;
The tatters drummed the devil's tattoo. On
The buckling yard a block thumped like a mall.
The ship lay — the sea smote her, the wind's bawl
Came, "loo, loo, loo!" The devil cried his hounds
On to the poor spent stag strayed in his bounds.

"Cut! Ease her!" yelled his mate; the Dauber heard
His mate wormed up the tilted yard and slashed,
A rag of canvas skimmed like a darting bird.

The snow whirled, the ship bowed to it, the gear lashed,
The sea-tops were cut off and flung down smashed;
Tatters of shouts were flung, the rags of yells —
And clang, clang, clang, below beat the two bells.

"O God!" the Dauber moaned. A roaring rang,
Blasting the royals like a cannonade;
The backstays parted with a cracking clang,
The upper spars were snapped like twigs decayed —
Snapped at their heels, their jagged splinters splayed,
Like white and ghastly hair erect with fear.
The Mate yelled, "Gone, by God, and pitched them
    clear!"

"Up!" yelled the Bosun; "up and clear the wreck!"
The Dauber followed where he led : below
He caught one giddy glimpsing of the deck
Filled with white water, as though heaped with snow.
He saw the streamers of the rigging blow
Straight out like pennons from the splintered mast,
Then, all sense dimmed, all was an icy blast

Roaring from nether hell and filled with ice,
Roaring and crashing on the jerking stage,
An utter bridle given to utter vice,
Limitless power mad with endless rage
Withering the soul; a minute seemed an age.
He clutched and hacked at ropes, at rags of sail,
Thinking that comfort was a fairy-tale

Told long ago — long, long ago — long since
Heard of in other lives — imagined, dreamed —
There where the basest beggar was a prince
To him in torment where the tempest screamed,
Comfort and warmth and ease no longer seemed
Things that a man could know: soul, body, brain,
Knew nothing but the wind, the cold, the pain.

"Leave that!" the Bosun shouted; "Crojick save!"
The splitting crojick, not yet gone to rags,
Thundered below, beating till something gave,
Bellying between its buntlines into bags.
Some birds were blown past, shrieking: dark, like
    shags,
Their backs seemed, looking down. "Leu, leu!" they
    cried.
The ship lay, the seas thumped her; she had died.

They reached the crojick yard, which buckled, buckled
Like a thin whalebone to the topsail's strain.
They laid upon the yard and heaved and knuckled,
Pounding the sail, which jangled and leapt again.
It was quite hard with ice, its rope like chain,
Its strength like seven devils; it shook the mast.
They cursed and toiled and froze: a long time passed.

Two hours passed, then a dim lightening came.
Those frozen ones upon the yard could see
The mainsail and the foresail still the same,

H

Still battling with the hands and blowing free,
Rags tattered where the staysails used to be.
The lower topsails stood; the ship's lee deck
Seethed with four feet of water filled with wreck.

An hour more went by; the Dauber lost
All sense of hands and feet, all sense of all
But of a wind that cut him to the ghost,
And of a frozen fold he had to haul,
Of heavens that fell and never ceased to fall,
And ran in smoky snatches along the sea,
Leaping from crest to wave-crest, yelling. He

Lost sense of time; no bells went, but he felt
Ages go over him. At last, at last
They frapped the cringled crojick's icy pelt;
In frozen bulge and bunt they made it fast.
Then, scarcely live, they laid in to the mast.
The Captain's speaking trumpet gave a blare,
"Make fast the topsail, Mister, while you're there."

Some seamen cursed, but up they had to go —
Up to the topsail yard to spend an hour
Stowing a topsail in a blinding snow,
Which made the strongest man among them cower.
More men came up, the fresh hands gave them power,
They stowed the sail; then with a rattle of chain
One half the crojick burst its bonds again.

*   *   *   *   *   *   *

They stowed the sail, frapping it round with rope,
Leaving no surface for the wind, no fold,
Then down the weather shrouds, half dead, they
    grope;
That struggle with the sail had made them old.
They wondered if the crojick furl would hold.
"Lucky," said one, "it didn't spring the spar."
"Lucky!" the Bosun said, "Lucky! We are!

She came within two shakes of turning top
Or stripping all her shroud-screws, that first quiff.
Now fish those wash-deck buckets out of the slop.
Here's Dauber says he doesn't like Cape Stiff.
This isn't wind, man, this is only a whiff.
Hold on, all hands, hold on!" a sea, half seen,
Paused, mounted, burst, and filled the main-deck
    green.

The Dauber felt a mountain of water fall.
It covered him deep, deep, he felt it fill,
Over his head, the deck, the fife-rails, all,
Quieting the ship, she trembled and lay still.
Then with a rush and shatter and clanging shrill
Over she went; he saw the water cream
Over the bitts; he saw the half-deck stream.

Then in the rush he swirled, over she went;
Her lee-rail dipped, he struck, and something gave;
His legs went through a port as the roll spent;
She paused, then rolled, and back the water drave.

He drifted with it as a part of the wave,
Drowning, half-stunned, exhausted, partly frozen,
He struck the booby hatchway; then the Bosun.

Leaped, seeing his chance, before the next sea burst,
And caught him as he drifted, seized him, held,
Up-ended him against the bitts, and cursed.
"This ain't the George's Swimming Baths," he yelled;
"Keep on your feet!"   Another grey-back felled
The two together, and the Bose, half-blind,
Spat: "One's a joke," he cursed, "but two's unkind."

"Now, damn it, Dauber!" said the Mate.   "Look out,
Or you'll be over the side!"   The water freed;
Each clanging freeing-port became a spout.
The men cleared up the decks as there was need.
The Dauber's head was cut, he felt it bleed
Into his oilskins as he clutched and coiled.
Water and sky were devils' brews which boiled,

Boiled, shrieked, and glowered; but the ship was saved.
Snugged safely down, though fourteen sails were split.
Out of the dark a fiercer fury raved.
The grey-backs died and mounted, each crest lit
With a white toppling gleam that hissed from it
And slid, or leaped, or ran with whirls of cloud,
Mad with inhuman life that shrieked aloud.

The watch was called; Dauber might go below.
"Splice the main brace!" the Mate called.   All laid aft

To get a gulp of momentary glow
As some reward for having saved the craft.
The steward ladled mugs, from which each quaff'd
Whisky, with water, sugar, and lime-juice, hot,
A quarter of a pint each made the tot.

Beside the lamp-room door the steward stood
Ladling it out, and each man came in turn,
Tipped his sou'-wester, drank it, grunted "Good!"
And shambled forward, letting it slowly burn:
When all were gone the Dauber lagged astern,
Torn by his frozen body's lust for heat,
The liquor's pleasant smell, so warm, so sweet,

And by a promise long since made at home
Never to taste strong liquor. Now he knew
The worth of liquor; now he wanted some.
His frozen body urged him to the brew;
Yet it seemed wrong, an evil thing to do
To break that promise. "Dauber," said the Mate,
"Drink, and turn in, man; why the hell d'ye wait?"

"Please, sir, I'm temperance." "Temperance are you, hey?
That's all the more for me! So you're for slops?
I thought you'd had enough slops for to-day.
Go to your bunk and ease her when she drops.
And — damme, steward! you brew with too much hops
Stir up the sugar, man! — and tell your girl
How kind the Mate was teaching you to furl."

Then the Mate drank the remnants, six men's share
And ramped into his cabin, where he stripped
And danced unclad, and was uproarious there.
In waltzes with the cabin cat he tripped,
Singing in tenor clear that he was pipped —
That "he who strove the tempest to disarm,
Must never first embrail the lee yard-arm,"

And that his name was Ginger. Dauber crept
Back to the round-house, gripping by the rail.
The wind howled by; the passionate water leapt;
The night was all one roaring with the gale.
Then at the door he stopped, uttering a wail;
His hands were perished numb and blue as veins,
He could not turn the knob for both the Spains.

A hand came shuffling aft, dodging the seas,
Singing "her nut-brown hair" between his teeth;
Taking the ocean's tumult at his ease
Even when the wash about his thighs did seethe.
His soul was happy in its happy sheath;
"What, Dauber, won't it open?   Fingers cold?
You'll talk of this time, Dauber, when you're old."

He flung the door half open, and a sea
Washed them both in, over the splash-board, down;
"You silly, salt miscarriage!" sputtered he.
"Dauber, pull out the plug before we drown!
That's spoiled my laces and my velvet gown.

Where is the plug?" Groping in pitch dark water,
He sang between his teeth "The Farmer's Daughter."

It was pitch dark within there; at each roll
The chests slid to the slant; the water rushed,
Making full many a clanging tin pan bowl
Into the black below-bunks as it gushed.
The dog-tired men slept through it; they were hushed.
The water drained, and then with matches damp
The man struck heads off till he lit the lamp.

"Thank you," the Dauber said; the seaman grinned.
"This is your first foul weather?" "Yes." "I thought
Up on the yard you hadn't seen much wind.
Them's rotten sea-boots, Dauber, that you brought.
Now I must cut on deck before I'm caught."
He went; the lamp-flame smoked; he slammed the door;
A film of water loitered across the floor.

The Dauber watched it come and watched it go;
He had had revelation of the lies
Cloaking the truth men never choose to know;
He could bear witness now and cleanse their eyes.
He had beheld in suffering; he was wise;
This was the sea, this searcher of the soul —
This never-dying shriek fresh from the Pole.

He shook with cold; his hands could not undo
His oilskin buttons, so he shook and sat,

Watching his dirty fingers, dirty blue,
Hearing without the hammering tackle slat,
Within, the drops from dripping clothes went pat,
Running in little patters, gentle, sweet,
And "Ai, ai!" went the wind, and the seas beat.

His bunk was sopping wet; he clambered in.
None of his clothes were dry; his fear recurred.
Cramps bunched the muscles underneath his skin.
The great ship rolled until the lamp was blurred.
He took his Bible and tried to read a word;
Trembled at going aloft again, and then
Resolved to fight it out and show it to men.

Faces recurred, fierce memories of the yard,
The frozen sail, the savage eyes, the jests,
The oaths of one great seaman, syphilis-scarred,
The tug of leeches jammed beneath their chests,
The buntlines bellying bunts out into breasts.
The deck so desolate-grey, the sky so wild,
He fell asleep, and slept like a young child.

But not for long; the cold awoke him soon,
The hot-ache and the skin-cracks and the cramp,
The seas thundering without, the gale's wild tune.
The sopping misery of the blankets damp.
A speaking-trumpet roared; a sea-boot's stamp
Clogged at the door. A man entered to shout:
"All hands on deck! Arouse here! Tumble out!"

The caller raised the lamp; his oilskins clicked
As the thin ice upon them cracked and fell.
"Rouse out!" he said. "This lamp is frozen wick'd.
Rouse out!" His accent deepened to a yell.
"We're among ice; it's blowing up like hell.
We're going to hand both topsails. Time, I guess,
We're sheeted up. Rouse out! Don't stay to dress!"

"Is it cold on deck?" said Dauber. "Is it cold?
We're sheeted up, I tell you, inches thick!
The fo'c'sle's like a wedding-cake, I'm told.
Now tumble out, my sons; on deck here, quick!
Rouse out, away, and come and climb the stick.
I'm going to call the half-deck. Bosun! Hey!
Both topsails coming in. Heave out! Away!"

He went; the Dauber tumbled from his bunk,
Clutching the side. He heard the wind go past,
Making the great ship wallow as if drunk.
There was a shocking tumult up the mast.
"This is the end," he muttered, "come at last!
I've got to go aloft, facing this cold.
I can't. I can't. I'll never keep my hold.

"I cannot face the topsail yard again.
I never guessed what misery it would be."
The cramps and hot-ache made him sick with pain
The ship stopped suddenly from a devilish sea,
Then, with a triumph of wash, a rush of glee,

The door burst in, and in the water rolled,
Filling the lower bunks, black, creaming, cold.

The lamp sucked out. "Wash!" went the water back,
Then in again, flooding; the Bosun swore.
"You useless thing! You Dauber! You lee slack!
Get out, you heekapoota! Shut the door!
You coo-ilyaira, what are you waiting for?
Out of my way, you thing — you useless thing!"
He slammed the door indignant, clanging the ring.

And then he lit the lamp, drowned to the waist;
"Here's a fine house! Get at the scupper-holes" —
He bent against it as the water raced —
"And pull them out to leeward when she rolls.
They say some kinds of landsmen don't have souls.
I well believe. A Port Mahon baboon
Would make more soul than you got with a spoon."

Down in the icy water Dauber groped
To find the plug; the racing water sluiced
Over his head and shoulders as she sloped.
Without, judged by the sound, all hell was loosed.
He felt cold Death about him tightly noosed.
That Death was better than the misery there
Iced on the quaking foothold high in air.

And then the thought came: "I'm a failure. All
My life has been a failure. They were right.

It will not matter if I go and fall;
I should be free then from this hell's delight.
I'll never paint.   Best let it end to-night.
I'll slip over the side.   I've tried and failed."
So in the ice-cold in the night he quailed.

Death would be better, death, than this long hell
Of mockery and surrender and dismay —
This long defeat of doing nothing well,
Playing the part too high for him to play.
"O Death! who hides the sorry thing away,
Take me; I've failed.   I cannot play these cards."
There came a thundering from the topsail yards.

And then he bit his lips, clenching his mind,
And staggered out to muster, beating back
The coward frozen self of him that whined.
Come what cards might he meant to play the pack.
"Ai!" screamed the wind; the topsail sheet went clack;
Ice filled the air with spikes; the greybacks burst.
"Here's Dauber," said the Mate, "on deck the first.

"Why, holy sailor, Dauber, you're a man!
I took you for a soldier.   Up now, come!"
Up on the yards already they began
That battle with a gale which strikes men dumb.
The leaping topsail thundered like a drum.
The frozen snow beat in the face like shots.
The wind spun whipping wave-crests into clots.

So up upon the topsail yard again,
In the great tempest's fiercest hour, began
Probation to the Dauber's soul, of pain
Which crowds a century's torment in a span.
For the next month the ocean taught this man,
And he, in that month's torment, while she wested.
Was never warm nor dry, nor full nor rested.

But still it blew, or, if it lulled, it rose
Within the hour and blew again; and still
The water as it burst aboard her froze.
The wind blew off an ice-field, raw and chill,
Daunting man's body, tampering with his will;
But after thirty days a ghostly sun
Gave sickly promise that the storms were done.

———

The Captain eyed her aft, sucking his lip,
Feeling the sail too much, but yet refraining
From putting hobbles on the leaping ship,
The glad sea-shattering stallion, halter-straining,
Wing-musical, uproarious, and complaining;
But, in a gust, he cocked his finger, so:
"You'd better take them off, before they go."

All saw.   They ran at once without the word
"Lee-ay!   Lee-ay!"   Loud rang the clewline cries;
Sam in his bunk within the half-deck heard,
Stirred in his sleep, and rubbed his drowsy eyes.

"There go the lower to 'gallants." Against the skies
Rose the thin bellying strips of leaping sail.
The Dauber was the first man over the rail.

Three to a mast they ran; it was a race.
"God!" said the Mate; "that Dauber, he can go."
He watched the runners with an upturned face
Over the futtocks, struggling heel to toe,
Up to the topmast cross-trees into the blow
Where the three sails were leaping. "Dauber wins!"
The yards were reached, and now the race begins.

Which three will furl their sail first and come down?
Out to the yard-arm for the leech goes one,
His hair blown flagwise from a hatless crown,
His hands at work like fever to be done.
Out of the gale a fiercer fury spun.
The three sails leaped together, yanking high,
Like talons darting up to clutch the sky.

The Dauber on the fore-topgallant yard
Out at the weather yard-arm was the first
To lay his hand upon the buntline-barred
Topgallant yanking to the wester's burst;
He craned to catch the leech; his comrades cursed;
One at the buntlines, one with oaths observed,
"The eye of the outer jib-stay isn't served."

"No," said the Dauber. "No," the man replied.
They heaved, stowing the sail, not looking round,

Panting, but full of life and eager-eyed;
The gale roared at them with its iron sound.
"That's you," the Dauber said. His gasket wound
Swift round the yard, binding the sail in bands;
There came a gust, the sail leaped from his hands,

So that he saw it high above him, grey,
And there his mate was falling; quick he clutched
An arm in oilskins swiftly snatched away.
A voice said "Christ!" a quick shape stooped and touched,
Chain struck his hands, ropes shot, the sky was smutched
With vast black fires that ran, that fell, that furled,
And then he saw the mast, the small snow hurled,

The fore-topgallant yard far, far aloft,
And blackness settling on him and great pain;
And snow beneath his fingers wet and soft,
And topsail sheet-blocks shaking at the chain.
He knew it was he who had fallen; then his brain
Swirled in a circle while he watched the sky.
Infinite multitudes of snow blew by.

"I thought it was Tom who fell," his brain's voice said.
"Down on the bloody deck!" the Captain screamed.
The multitudinous little snow-flakes sped.
His pain was real enough, but all else seemed.
Si with a bucket ran, the water gleamed
Tilting upon him; others came, the Mate . . .
They knelt with eager eyes like things that wait

For other things to come.   He saw them there.
"It will go on," he murmured, watching Si.
Colours and sounds seemed mixing in the air,
The pain was stunning him, and the wind went by.
"More water," said the Mate.   "Here, Bosun, try.
Ask if he's got a message.   Hell, he's gone!
Here, Dauber, paints."   He said, "It will go on."

Not knowing his meaning rightly, but he spoke
With the intenseness of a fading soul
Whose share of Nature's fire turns to smoke,
Whose hand on Nature's wheel loses control.
The eager faces glowered red like coal.
They glowed, the great storm glowed, the sails, the
        mast.
"It will go on," he cried aloud, and passed.

Those from the yard came down to tell the tale.
"He almost had me off," said Tom.   "He slipped.
There came one hell of a jump-like from the sail. . . .
He clutched at me and almost had me pipped.
He caught my 'ris'band, but the oilskin ripped. . . .
It tore clean off.   Look here.   I was near gone.
I made a grab to catch him; so did John.

"I caught his arm.   My God!   I was near done.
He almost had me over; it was near.
He hit the ropes and grabbed at every one."
"Well," said the Mate, "we cannot leave him here.

Run, Si, and get the half-deck table clear.
We'll lay him there. Catch hold there, you, and you,
He's dead, poor son; there's nothing more to do."

Night fell, and all night long the Dauber lay
Covered upon the table; all night long
The pitiless storm exulted at her prey,
Huddling the waters with her icy thong.
But to the covered shape she did no wrong.
He lay beneath the sailcloth. Bell by bell
The night wore through; the stars rose, the stars fell.

Blowing most pitiless cold out of clear sky
The wind roared all night long; and all night through
The green seas on the deck went washing by,
Flooding the half-deck; bitter hard it blew.
But little of it all the Dauber knew —
The sopping bunks, the floating chests, the wet,
The darkness, and the misery, and the sweat.

He was off duty. So it blew all night,
And when the watches changed the men would come
Dripping within the door to strike a light
And stare upon the Dauber lying dumb,
And say, "He come a cruel thump, poor chum."
Or, "He'd a-been a fine big man;" or, "He . . .
A smart young seaman he was getting to be."

Or, "Damn it all, it's what we've all to face! . .
I knew another fellow one time . . ." then

Came a strange tale of death in a strange place
Out on the sea, in ships, with wandering men.
In many ways Death puts us into pen.
The reefers came down tired and looked and slept.
Below the skylight little dribbles crept

Along the painted woodwork, glistening, slow,
Following the roll and dripping, never fast,
But dripping on the quiet form below,
Like passing time talking to time long past.
And all night long "Ai, ai!" went the wind's blast,
And creaming water swished below the pale,
Unheeding body stretched beneath the sail.

At dawn they sewed him up, and at eight bells
They bore him to the gangway, wading deep,
Through the green-clutching, white-toothed water-hells
That flung his carriers over in their sweep
They laid an old red ensign on the heap,
And all hands stood bare-headed, stooping, swaying,
Washed by the sea while the old man was praying

Out of a borrowed prayer-book. At a sign
They twitched the ensign back and tipped the grating.
A creamier bubbling broke the bubbling brine.
The muffled figure tilted to the weighting;
It dwindled slowly down, slowly gyrating.
Some craned to see; it dimmed, it disappeared;
The last green milky bubble blinked and cleared.

"Mister, shake out your reefs," the Captain called.
"Out topsail reefs!" the Mate cried; then all hands
Hurried, the great sails shook, and all hands hauled,
Singing that desolate song of lonely lands,
Of how a lover came in dripping bands,
Green with the wet and cold, to tell his lover
That Death was in the sea, and all was over.

Fair came the falling wind; a seaman said
The Dauber was a Jonah; once again
The clipper held her course, showing red lead,
Shattering the sea-tops into golden rain.
The waves bowed down before her like blown grain;
Onwards she thundered, on; her voyage was short,
Before the tier's bells rang her into port.

Cheerly they rang her in, those beating bells,
The new-come beauty stately from the sea,
Whitening the blue heave of the drowsy swells,
Treading the bubbles down. With three times three
They cheered her moving beauty in, and she
Came to her berth so noble, so superb;
Swayed like a queen, and answered to the curb.

Then in the sunset's flush they went aloft.
And unbent sails in that most lovely hour,
When the light gentles and the wind is soft,
And beauty in the heart breaks like a flower.
Working aloft they saw the mountain tower.

Snow to the peak; they heard the launchmen shout;
And bright along the bay the lights came out.

And then the night fell dark, and all night long
The pointed mountain pointed at the stars,
Frozen, alert, austere; the eagle's song
Screamed from her desolate screes and splintered scars.
On her intense crags where the air is sparse
The stars looked down; their many golden eyes
Watched her and burned, burned out, and came to rise.

Silent the finger of the summit stood,
Icy in pure, thin air, glittering with snows.
Then the sun's coming turned the peak to blood,
And in the rest-house the muleteers arose.
And all day long, where only the eagle goes,
Stones, loosened by the sun, fall; the stones falling
Fill empty gorge on gorge with echoes calling.

FROM *BIOGRAPHY*

DAYS of endeavour have been good: the days
Racing in cutters or the comrade's praise,
The day they led my cutter at the turn
Yet could not keep the lead and dropped astern,
The moment in the spurt when both boats' oars
Dipped in each other's wash and throats grew hoarse
And teeth ground into teeth and both strokes quick-
    ened
Lashing the sea, and gasps came, and hearts sickened
And coxswains damned us, dancing, banking stroke,
To put our weights on, though our hearts were broke
And both boats seemed to stick and sea seemed glue,
The tide a mill race we were struggling through
And every quick recover gave us squints
Of them still there, and oar tossed waterglints
And cheering came, our friends, our foemen cheering,
A long, wild, rallying murmur on the hearing —
"Port Fore!" and "Starboard Fore!" "Port Fore."
    "Port Fore."
"Up with her, Starboard," and at that each oar
Lightened, though arms were bursting, and eyes shut
And the oak stretchers grunted in the strut
And the curse quickened from the cox, our bows

Lashing the sea, and gasps came, and hearts sickened
And coxswains damned us, dancing, banking stroke,
To put our weights on, though our hearts were broke
And both boats seemed to stick and sea seemed glue,
The tide a mill race we were struggling through.

Crashed, and drove talking water, we made vows,
Chastity vows and temperance; in our pain
We numbered things we'd never eat again
If we could only win; then came the yell
"Starboard," "Port Fore," and then a beaten bell
Rung as for fire to cheer us.   "Now."   Oars bent,
Soul took the looms now body's bolt was spent,
"Damn it, come on now," "On now," "On now," "Star-
    board."
"Port Fore."   "Up with her, Port"; each cutter har-
    boured
Ten eye-shut painsick strugglers, "Heave, oh, heave,"
Catcalls waked echoes like a shrieking sheave.
"Heave," and I saw a back, then two.   "Port Fore."
"Starboard."   "Come on."   I saw the midship oar
And knew we had done them.   "Port Fore."
"Starboard."   "Now."
I saw bright water spurting at their bow
Their cox' full face an instant.   They were done.
The watchers' cheering almost drowned the gun.
We had hardly strength to toss our oars; our cry
Cheering the losing cutter was a sigh.

SALT-WATER POEMS

THE SHIP AND HER MAKERS

THE ORE

BEFORE Man's labouring wisdom gave me birth
I had not even seen the light of day;
Down in the central darkness of the earth,
Crushed by the weight of continents I lay,
Ground by the weight to heat, not knowing then
The Air, the light, the noise, the world of men.

THE TREES

We grew on mountains where the glaciers cry,
Infinite sombre armies of us stood
Below the snow-peaks which defy the sky;
A song like the gods moaning filled our wood;
We knew no men — our life was to stand staunch,
Singing our song, against the avalanche.

THE HEMP AND FLAX

We were a million grasses on the hill,
A million herbs which bowed as the wind blew,
Trembling in every fibre, never still;
Out of the summer earth sweet life we drew.
Little blue-flowered grasses up the glen,
Glad of the sun, what did we know of men?

The Workers

We tore the iron from the mountain's hold,
By blasting fires we smithied it to steel;
Out of the shapeless stone we learned to mould
The sweeping bow, the rectilinear keel;
We hewed the pine to plank, we split the fir,
We pulled the myriad flax to fashion her.

Out of a million lives our knowledge came,
A million subtle craftsmen forged the means;
Steam was our handmaid and our servant flame,
Water our strength, all bowed to our machines.
Out of the rock, the tree, the springing herb
We built this wandering beauty so superb.

The Sailors

We, who were born on earth and live by air,
Make this thing pass across the fatal floor,
The speechless sea; alone we commune there
Jesting with death, that ever open door.
Sun, moon and stars are signs by which we drive
This wind-blown iron like a thing alive.

The Ship

I march across great waters like a queen,
I whom so many wisdoms helped to make;
Over the uncruddled billows of seas green
I blanch the bubbled highway of my wake.
By me my wandering tenants clasp the hands,
And know the thoughts of men in other lands.

THE NEW BEDFORD WHALER

THERE was a 'Bedford Whaler put out to hunt for oil,
With a try-works in amidships where chunks of whale
    could boil,
And a fo'c's'le, wet and frowsy, where whalers' crews
    could gam,
And her captain came from 'Bedford and did not give a
    cent,
So over the bar from 'Bedford to hunt the whale she went.

But never a whale she sighted for eight and forty moons,
She never lowered her boats in chase nor reddened her
    harpoons,
So home she went to 'Bedford, where her owners came to
    ask,
"How many tons of whalebone, cap, and how much oil
    in cask?"

The captain turned his tobacco inside his weather cheek,
And he said "At least the Bible says, blessed are they who
    seek.
We've been at sea four years and more and never seen a
    whale,
We haven't a lick of oil on board but we've had a darned
    good sail."

CARGOES

QUINQUIREME of Nineveh from distant Ophir,
Rowing home to haven in sunny Palestine,
With a cargo of ivory,
And apes and peacocks,
Sandalwood, cedarwood, and sweet white wine.

Stately Spanish galleon coming from the Isthmus,
Dipping through the Tropics by the palmgreen shores,
With a cargo of diamonds,
Emeralds, amethysts,
Topazes, and cinnamon, and gold moidores.

Dirty British coaster with a salt-caked smoke stack,
Butting through the Channel in the mad March days,
With a cargo of Tyne coal,
Road-rails, pig-lead,
Firewood, iron-ware, and cheap tin trays.

CAPTAIN STRATTON'S FANCY

Oh some are fond of red wine, and some are fond of
    white,
And some are all for dancing by the pale moonlight:
But rum alone's the tipple, and the heart's delight
    Of the old bold mate of Henry Morgan.

Oh some are fond of Spanish wine, and some are fond of
    French,
And some'll swallow tay and stuff fit only for a wench;
But I'm for right Jamaica till I roll beneath the bench,
    Says the old bold mate of Henry Morgan.

Oh some are for the lily, and some are for the rose,
But I am for the sugar-cane that in Jamaica grows;
For it's that that makes the bonny drink to warm my
    copper nose,
    Says the old bold mate of Henry Morgan.

Oh some are fond of fiddles, and a song well sung,
And some are all for music for to lilt upon the tongue;
But mouths were made for tankards, and for sucking at
    the bung,
    Says the old bold mate of Henry Morgan.

Oh some are fond of dancing, and some are fond of dice,
And some are all for red lips, and pretty lasses' eyes;
But a right Jamaica puncheon is a finer prize
  To the old bold mate of Henry Morgan.

Oh some that's good and godly ones they hold that it's a
    sin
To troll the jolly bowl around, and let the dollars spin;
But I'm for toleration and for drinking at an inn,
  Says the old bold mate of Henry Morgan.

Oh some are sad and wretched folk that go in silken suits,
And there's a mort of wicked rogues that live in good
    reputes;
So I'm for drinking honestly, and dying in my boots,
  Like an old bold mate of Henry Morgan.

THIRD MATE

ALL the sheets are clacking, all the blocks are whining,
The sails are frozen stiff and the wetted decks are shining:
The reef's in the topsails, and it's coming on to blow,
And I think of the dear girl I left long ago.

Grey were her eyes, and her hair was long and bonny,
Golden was her hair, like the wild bees' honey.
And I was but a dog, and a mad one to despise,
The gold of her hair and the grey of her eyes.

There's the sea before me, and my home's behind me,
And beyond there the strange lands where nobody will
    mind me,
No one but the girls with the paint upon their cheeks,
Who sell away their beauty to whomsoever seeks.

There'll be drink and women there, and songs and laughter,
Peace from what is past and from all that follows after;
And a fellow will forget how a woman lies awake,
Lonely in the night watch crying for his sake.

Black it blows and bad and it howls like slaughter,
And the ship she shudders as she takes the water.
Hissing flies the spindrift like a wind-blown smoke,
And I think of a woman and a heart I broke.

POSTED AS MISSING

Under all her topsails she trembled like a stag,
The wind made a ripple in her bonny red flag;
They cheered her from the shore and they cheered her
    from the pier,
And under all her topsails she trembled like a deer.

So she passed swaying, where the green seas run,
Her wind-steadied topsails were stately in the sun;
There was glitter on the water from her red port light,
So she passed swaying, till she was out of sight.

Long and long ago it was, a weary time it is,
The bones of her sailor-men are coral plants by this;
Coral plants, and shark-weed, and a mermaid's comb,
And if the fishers net them they never bring them home.

It's rough on sailors' women. They have to mangle hard,
And stitch at dungarees till their finger-ends are scarred,
Thinking of the sailor-men who sang among the crowd,
Hoisting of her topsails when she sailed so proud.

SHIPS

I CANNOT tell their wonder nor make known
Magic that once thrilled through me to the bone,
But all men praise some beauty, tell some tale,
Vent a high mood which makes the rest seem pale,
Pour their heart's blood to flourish one green leaf,
Follow some Helen for her gift of grief,
And fail in what they mean, whate'er they do:
You should have seen, man cannot tell to you
The beauty of the ships of that my city.

That beauty now is spoiled by the sea's pity;
For one may haunt the pier a score of times,
Hearing St. Nicholas bells ring out the chimes,
Yet never see those proud ones swaying home
With mainyards backed and bows a cream of foam,
Those bows so lovely-curving, cut so fine,
Those coulters of the many-bubbled brine,
As once, long since, when all the docks were filled
With that sea-beauty man has ceased to build

Yet, though their splendour may have ceased to be,
Each played her sovereign part in making me;
Now I return my thanks with heart and lips
For the great queenliness of all those ships.

And first the first bright memory, still so clear,
An autumn evening in a golden year,
When in the last lit moments before dark
The *Chepica*, a steel-grey lovely barque,
Came to an anchor near us on the flood,
Her trucks aloft in sun-glow red as blood.

Then come so many ships that I could fill
Three docks with their fair hulls remembered still,
Each with her special memory's special grace,
Riding the sea, making the waves give place
To delicate high beauty; man's best strength,
Noble in every line in all their length.
Ailsa, *Genista*, ships, with long jibbooms,
The *Wanderer* with great beauty and strange dooms,
Liverpool (mightiest then) superb, sublime,
The *California* huge, as slow as time.
The *Copley* swift, the perfect *J. T. North*,
The loveliest barque my city has sent forth,
Dainty *John Lockett* well remembered yet,
The splendid *Argus* with her skysail set,
Stalwart *Drumcliff*, white-blocked, majestic *Sierras*,
Divine bright ships, the water's standard-bearers ·
Melpomene, *Euphrosyne*, and their sweet
Sea-troubling sisters of the Fernie fleet;
Corunna (in whom my friend died) and the old
Long since loved *Esmeralda* long since sold.
Centurion passed in Rio, *Glaucus* spoken,
Aladdin burnt, the *Bidston* water-broken,

Yola, in whom my friend sailed, *Dawpool* trim,
Fierce bowed *Egeria* plunging to the swim,
Stanmore wide-sterned, sweet *Cupica*, tall *Bard*,
Queen in all harbours with her moon sail yard.

Though I tell many, there must still be others,
McVickar Marshall's ships and Fernie Brothers',
Lochs, Counties, Shires, Drums, the countless lines
Whose house-flags all were once familiar signs
At high main-trucks on Mersey's windy ways
When sunlight made the wind-white water blaze.
Their names bring back old mornings, when the docks
Shone with their house-flags and their painted blocks,
Their raking masts below the Custom House
And all the marvellous beauty of their bows.

Familiar steamers, too, majestic steamers,
Shearing Atlantic roller-tops to streamers,
Umbria, Etruria, noble, still at sea,
The grandest, then, that man had brought to be.
Majestic, City of Paris, City of Rome,
Forever jealous racers, out and home.
The *Alfred Holt's* blue smoke-stacks down the stream,
The fair *Loanda* with her bows a-cream.
Booth liners, Anchor liners, Red Star liners,
The marks and styles of countless ship-designers,
The *Magdalena, Puno, Potosi*,
Lost *Cotopaxi*, all well known to me.

These splendid ships, each with her grace, her glory,
Her memory of old song or comrade's story,
Still in my mind the image of life's need,
Beauty in hardest action, beauty indeed.
"'They built great ships and sailed them" sounds most
    brave
Whatever arts we have or fail to have;
I touch my country's mind, I come to grips
With half her purpose, thinking of these ships,
That art untouched by softness, all that line
Drawn ringing hard to stand the test of brine,
That nobleness and grandeur, all that beauty
Born of a manly life and bitter duty,
That splendour of fine bows which yet could stand
The shock of rollers never checked by land.
That art of masts, sail crowded, fit to break,
Yet stayed to strength and backstayed into rake,
The life demanded by that art, the keen
Eye-puckered, hard-case seamen, silent, lean, —
They are grander things than all the art of towns,
Their tests are tempests and the sea that drowns,
They are my country's line, her great art done
By strong brains labouring on the thought unwon,
They mark our passage as a race of men,
Earth will not see such ships as those again.

ROADWAYS

ONE road leads to London,
  One road runs to Wales,
My road leads me seawards
  To the white dipping sails.

One road leads to the river,
  As it goes singing slow;
My road leads to shipping,
  Where the bronzed sailors go.

Leads me, lures me, calls me
  To salt green tossing sea;
A road without earth's road-dust
  Is the right road for me.

A wet road heaving, shining,
  And wild with seagulls' cries,
A mad salt sea-wind blowing
  The salt spray in my eyes.

My road calls me, lures me
  West, east, south, and north;

Most roads lead men homewards,
My road leads me forth

To add more miles to the tally
Of grey miles left behind,
In quest of that one beauty
God put me here to find.

THE "WANDERER"

ALL day they loitered by the resting ships,
Telling their beauties over, taking stock;
At night the verdict left my messmates' lips,
"The *Wanderer* is the finest ship in dock."

I had not seen her, but a friend, since drowned,
Drew her, with painted ports, low, lovely, lean,
Saying, "The *Wanderer*, clipper, outward bound,
The loveliest ship my eyes have ever seen —

"Perhaps to-morrow you will see her sail.
She sails at sunrise": but the morrow showed
No *Wanderer* setting forth for me to hail;
Far down the stream men pointed where she rode,

Rode the great trackway to the sea, dim, dim,
Already gone before the stars were gone.
I saw her at the sea-line's smoky rim
Grow swiftly vaguer as they towed her on.

Soon even her masts were hidden in the haze
Beyond the city; she was on her course
To trample billows for a hundred days;
That afternoon the norther gathered force,

Blowing a small snow from a point of east.
"Oh, fair for her," we said, "to take her south."
And in our spirits, as the wind increased,
We saw her there, beyond the river mouth,

Setting her side-lights in the wildering dark,
To glint upon mad water, while the gale
Roared like a battle, snapping like a shark,
And drunken seamen struggled with the sail.

While with sick hearts her mates put out of mind
Their little children left astern, ashore,
And the gale's gathering made the darkness blind,
Water and air one intermingled roar.

Then we forgot her, for the fiddlers played,
Dancing and singing held our merry crew;
The old ship moaned a little as she swayed.
It blew all night, oh, bitter hard it blew!

So that at midnight I was called on deck
To keep an anchor-watch: I heard the sea
Roar past in white procession filled with wreck;
Intense bright frosty stars burned over me,

And the Greek brig beside us dipped and dipped,
White to the muzzle like a half-tide rock,
Drowned to the mainmast with the seas she shipped;
Her cable-swivels clanged at every shock.

And like a never-dying force, the wind
Roared till we shouted with it, roared until
Its vast vitality of wrath was thinned,
Had beat its fury breathless and was still.

By dawn the gale had dwindled into flaw,
A glorious morning followed: with my friend
I climbed the fo'c's'le-head to see; we saw
The waters hurrying shorewards without end.

Haze blotted out the river's lowest reach;
Out of the gloom the steamers, passing by,
Called with their sirens, hooting their sea-speech;
Out of the dimness others made reply.

And as we watched, there came a rush of feet
Charging the fo'c's'le till the hatchway shook.
Men all about us thrust their way, or beat,
Crying, "The *Wanderer!* Down the river! Look!"

I looked with them towards the dimness; there
Gleamed like a spirit striding out of night,
A full-rigged ship unutterably fair,
Her masts like trees in winter, frosty-bright.

Foam trembled at her bows like wisps of wool;
She trembled as she towed. I had not dreamed
That work of man could be so beautiful,
In its own presence and in what it seemed.

"So, she is putting back again," I said.
"How white with frost her yards are on the fore."
One of the men about me answer made,
"That is not frost, but all her sails are tore,

"Torn into tatters, youngster, in the gale;
Her best foul-weather suit gone." It was true,
Her masts were white with rags of tattered sail
Many as gannets when the fish are due.

Beauty in desolation was her pride,
Her crowned array a glory that had been;
She faltered tow'rds us like a swan that died,
But although ruined she was still a queen.

"Put back with all her sails gone," went the word;
Then, from her signals flying, rumour ran,
"The sea that stove her boats in killed her third;
She has been gutted and has lost a man."

So, as though stepping to a funeral march,
She passed defeated homewards whence she came,
Ragged with tattered canvas white as starch,
A wild bird that misfortune had made tame.

She was refitted soon: another took
The dead man's office; then the singers hove
Her capstan till the snapping hawsers shook;
Out, with a bubble at her bows, she drove.

Again they towed her seawards, and again
We, watching, praised her beauty, praised her trim,
Saw her fair house-flag flutter at the main,
And slowly saunter seawards, dwindling dim;

And wished her well, and wondered, as she died,
How, when her canvas had been sheeted home,
Her quivering length would sweep into her stride,
Making the greenness milky with her foam.

But when we rose next morning, we discerned
Her beauty once again a shattered thing;
Towing to dock the *Wanderer* returned,
A wounded sea-bird with a broken wing.

A spar was gone, her rigging's disarray
Told of a worse disaster than the last;
Like draggled hair dishevelled hung the stay,
Drooping and beating on the broken mast.

Half-mast upon her flagstaff hung her flag;
Word went among us how the broken spar
Had gored her captain like an angry stag,
And killed her mate a half-day from the bar.

She passed to dock upon the top of flood.
An old man near me shook his head and swore:
"Like a bad woman, she has tasted blood —
There'll be no trusting in her any more."

We thought it truth, and when we saw her there
Lying in dock, beyond, across the stream,
We would forget that we had called her fair,
We thought her murderess and the past a dream.

And when she sailed again, we watched in awe,
Wondering what bloody act her beauty planned,
What evil lurked behind the thing we saw,
What strength was there that thus annulled man's hand,

How next its triumph would compel man's will
Into compliance with external Fate,
How next the powers would use her to work ill
On suffering men; we had not long to wait.

For soon the outcry of derision rose,
"Here comes the *Wanderer!*" the expected cry.
Guessing the cause, our mockings joined with those
Yelled from the shipping as they towed her by.

She passed us close, her seamen paid no heed
To what was called: they stood, a sullen group,
Smoking and spitting, careless of her need,
Mocking the orders given from the poop.

Her mates and boys were working her; we stared.
What was the reason of this strange return,
This third annulling of the thing prepared?
No outward evil could our eyes discern.

Only like one who having formed a plan
Beyond the pitch of common minds, she sailed,
Mocked and deserted by the common man,
Made half divine to me for having failed.

We learned the reason soon; below the town
A stay had parted like a snapping reed,
"Warning," the men thought, "not to take her down."
They took the omen, they would not proceed.

Days passed before another crew would sign.
The *Wanderer* lay in dock alone, unmanned,
Feared as a thing possessed by powers malign,
Bound under curses not to leave the land.

But under passing Time fear passes too;
That terror passed, the sailors' hearts grew bold.
We learned in time that she had found a crew
And was bound out and southwards as of old.

And in contempt we thought, "A little while
Will bring her back again, dismantled, spoiled.
It is herself; she cannot change her style;
She has the habit now of being foiled."

So when a ship appeared among the haze,
We thought, "The *Wanderer* back again"; but no,
No *Wanderer* showed for many, many days,
Her passing lights made other waters glow.

But we would often think and talk of her,
Tell newer hands her story, wondering, then,
Upon what ocean she was *Wanderer*,
Bound to the cities built by foreign men.

And one by one our little conclave thinned,
Passed into ships and sailed and so away,
To drown in some great roaring of the wind,
Wanderers themselves, unhappy fortune's prey.

And Time went by me making memory dim,
Yet still I wondered if the *Wanderer* fared
Still pointing to the unreached ocean's rim,
Brightening the water where her breast was bared.

And much in ports abroad I eyed the ships,
Hoping to see her well-remembered form
Come with a curl of bubbles at her lips
Bright to her berth, the sovereign of the storm.

I never did, and many years went by,
Then, near a Southern port, one Christmas Eve,
I watched a gale go roaring through the sky,
Making the caldrons of the clouds upheave.

Then the wrack tattered and the stars appeared,
Millions of stars that seemed to speak in fire;
A byre cock cried aloud that morning neared,
The swinging wind-vane flashed upon the spire.

And soon men looked upon a glittering earth,
Intensely sparkling like a world new-born;
Only to look was spiritual birth,
So bright the raindrops ran along the thorn.

So bright they were, that one could almost pass
Beyond their twinkling to the source, and know
The glory pushing in the blade of grass,
That hidden soul which makes the flowers grow.

That soul was there apparent, not revealed,
Unearthly meanings covered every tree,
That wet grass grew in an immortal field,
Those waters fed some never-wrinkled sea.

The scarlet berries in the hedge stood out
Like revelations but the tongue unknown;
Even in the brooks a joy was quick: the trout
Rushed in a dumbness dumb to me alone.

All of the valley was aloud with brooks;
I walked the morning, breasting up the fells,
Taking again lost childhood from the rooks,
Whose cawing came above the Christmas bells.

I had not walked that glittering world before,
But up the hill a prompting came to me,
"This line of upland runs along the shore:
Beyond the hedgerow I shall see the sea."

And on the instant from beyond away
That long familiar sound, a ship's bell, broke
The hush below me in the unseen bay.
Old memories came: that inner prompting spoke.

And bright above the hedge a seagull's wings
Flashed and were steady upon empty air.
"A Power unseen," I cried, "prepares these things;
Those are her bells, the *Wanderer* is there."

So, hurrying to the hedge and looking down,
I saw a mighty bay's wind-crinkled blue
Ruffling the image of a tranquil town,
With lapsing waters glittering as they grew.

And near me in the road the shipping swung,
So stately and so still in such great peace
That like to drooping crests their colours hung,
Only their shadows trembled without cease.

I did but glance upon those anchored ships.
Even as my thought had told, I saw her plain;
Tense, like a supple athlete with lean hips,
Swiftness at pause, the *Wanderer* come again —

Come as of old a queen, untouched by Time,
Resting the beauty that no seas could tire,
Sparkling, as though the midnight's rain were rime,
Like a man's thought transfigured into fire.

And as I looked, one of her men began
To sing some simple tune of Christmas day;
Among her crew the song spread, man to man,
Until the singing rang across the bay;

And soon in other anchored ships the men
Joined in the singing with clear throats, until
The farm-boy heard it up the windy glen,
Above the noise of sheep-bells on the hill.

Over the water came the lifted song —
Blind pieces in a mighty game we swing;
Life's battle is a conquest for the strong;
The meaning shows in the defeated thing.

THE RIVER

ALL other waters have their time of peace,
Calm, or the turn of tide or summer drought;
But on these bars the tumults never cease,
In violent death this river passes out.

Brimming she goes, a bloody-coloured rush
Hurrying her heaped disorder, rank on rank,
Bubbleless speed so still that in the hush
One hears the mined earth dropping from the bank.

Slipping in little falls whose tingeings drown,
Sunk by the waves for ever pressing on.
Till with a stripping crash the tree goes down,
Its washing branches flounder and are gone.

Then, roaring out aloud, her water spreads,
Making a desolation where her waves
Shriek and give battle, tossing up their heads,
Tearing the shifting sandbanks into graves,

Changing the raddled ruin of her course
So swiftly, that the pilgrim on the shore
Hears the loud whirlpool laughing like a horse
Where the scurfed sand was parched an hour before.

And always underneath that heaving tide
The changing bottom runs, or piles, or quakes,
Flinging immense heaps up to wallow wide,
Sucking the surface into whirls like snakes.

If anything should touch that shifting sand,
All the blind bottom sucks it till it sinks;
It takes the clipper ere she comes to land,
It takes the thirsting tiger as he drinks.

And on the river pours — it never tires;
Blind, hungry, screaming, day and night the same
Purposeless hurry of a million ires,
Mad as the wind, as merciless as flame.

* * * * * * *

There was a full-rigged ship, the *Travancore*,
Towing to port against that river's rage —
A glittering ship made sparkling for the shore,
Taut to the pins in all her equipage.

Clanging, she topped the tide; her sails were furled,
Her men came loitering downwards from the yards;
They who had brought her half across the world,
Trampling so many billows into shards,

Now looking up, beheld their duty done,
The ship approaching port, the great masts bare,
Gaunt as three giants striding in the sun,
Proud, with the colours tailing out like hair.

So, having coiled their gear, they left the deck;
Within the fo'c'sle's gloom of banded steel,
Mottled like wood with many a painted speck,
They brought their plates and sat about a meal.

Then pushing back the tins, they lit their pipes,
Or slept, or played at cards, or gently spoke,
Light from the portholes shot in dusty stripes
Tranquilly moving, sometimes blue with smoke.

These sunbeams sidled when the vessel rolled,
Their lazy yellow dust-strips crossed the floor,
Lighting a man-hole leading to the hold,
A man-hole leaded down the day before.

Like gold the solder on the man-hole shone;
A few flies threading in a drowsy dance
Slept in their pattern, darted, and were gone.
The river roared against the ship's advance.

And quietly sleep came upon the crew,
Man by man drooped upon his arms and slept;
Without, the tugboat dragged the vessel through,
The rigging whined, the yelling water leapt,

Till blindly a careering wave's collapse
Rose from beneath her bows and spouted high
Spirting the fo'c'sle floor with noisy slaps:
A sleeper at the table heaved a sigh,

And lurched, half-drunk with sleep, across the floor.
Muttering and blinking like a man insane,
Cursed at the river's tumult, shut the door,
Blinked, and lurched back and fell asleep again.

Then there was greater silence in the room,
Ship's creakings ran along the beams and died,
The lazy sunbeams loitered up the gloom,
Stretching and touching till they reached the side.

*   *   *   *   *   *   *

Yet something jerking in the vessel's course
Told that the tug was getting her in hand
As, at a fence, one steadies down a horse,
To rush the whirlpool on Magellan Sand;

And in the uneasy water just below
Her Mate inquired "if the men should stir
And come on deck?" Her Captain answered "No,
Let them alone, the tug can manage her."

Then, as she settled down and gathered speed,
Her Mate inquired again "if they should come
Just to be ready there in case of need,
Since, on such godless bars, there might be some."

But "No," the Captain said, "the men have been
Boxing about since midnight, let them be.
The pilot's able and the ship's a queen,
The hands can rest until we come to quay."

They ceased, they took their stations; right ahead
The whirlpool heaped and sucked; in tenor tone
The steady leadsman chanted at the lead,
The ship crept forward trembling to the bone.

And just above the worst a passing wave
Brought to the line such unexpected stress
That as she tossed her bows her towrope gave,
Snapped at the collar like a stalk of cress.

Then, for a ghastly moment, she was loose,
Blind in the whirlpool, groping for a guide,
Swinging adrift without a moment's truce,
She struck the sand and fell upon her side.

And instantly the sand beneath her gave
So that she righted and again was flung,
Grinding the quicksand open for a grave,
Straining her masts until the steel was sprung.

The foremast broke; its mighty bulk of steel
Fell on the fo'c'sle door and jammed it tight;
The sand-rush heaped her to an even keel,
She settled down, resigned, she made no fight,

But, like an overladen beast, she lay
Dumb in the mud with billows at her lips,
Broken, where she had fallen in the way,
Grinding her grave among the bones of ships.

*   *   *   *   *   *   *

At the first crashing of the mast, the men
Sprang from their sleep to hurry to the deck;
They found that Fate had caught them in a pen,
The door that opened out was jammed with wreck.

Then, as, with shoulders down, their gathered strength
Hove on the door, but could not make it stir,
They felt the vessel tremble through her length;
The tug, made fast again, was plucking her.

Plucking, and causing motion, till it seemed
That she would get her off; they heard her screw
Mumble the bubbled rip-rap as she steamed;
"Please God, the tug will shift her!" said the crew.

"She's off!" the seamen said; they felt her glide,
Scraping the bottom with her bilge, until
Something collapsing clanged along her side;
The scraping stopped, the tugboat's screw was still.

"She's holed!" a voice without cried; "holed and
        jammed —
Holed on the old *Magellan*, sunk last June.
I lose my ticket and the men are damned;
They'll drown like rats unless we free them soon.

"My God, they shall not!" and the speaker beat
Blows with a crow upon the foremast's wreck;
Minute steel splinters fell about his feet,
No tremour stirred the ruin on the deck.

And as their natures bade, the seamen learned
That they were doomed within that buried door;
Some cursed, some raved, but one among them turned
Straight to the manhole leaded in the floor,

And sitting down astride it, drew his knife,
And staidly dug to pick away the lead,
While at the ports his fellows cried for life:
"Burst in the door, or we shall all be dead!"

For like a brook the leak below them clucked.
They felt the vessel settling; they could feel
How the blind bog beneath her gripped and sucked.
Their fingers beat their prison walls of steel.

And then the gurgling stopped — the ship was still.
She stayed; she sank no deeper — an arrest
Fothered the pouring leak; she ceased to fill.
She trod the mud, drowned only to the breast.

And probing at the well, the captain found
The leak no longer rising, so he cried:
"She is not sinking — you will not be drowned;
The shifting sand has silted up her side.

"Now there is time. The tug shall put ashore
And fetch explosives to us from the town:
I'll burst the house or blow away the door
(It will not kill you if you all lie down).

"Be easy in your minds, for you'll be free
As soon as we've the blast." The seamen heard
The tug go townwards, butting at the sea;
Some lit their pipes, the youngest of them cheered.

But still the digger bent above the lid,
Gouging the solder from it as at first,
Pecking the lead, intent on what he did;
The other seamen mocked at him or cursed.

And some among them nudged him as he picked.
He cursed them, grinning, but resumed his game;
His knife-point sometimes struck the lid and clicked.
The solder-pellets shone like silver flame.

And still his knife-blade clicked like ticking time
Counting the hour till the tug's return,
And still the ship stood steady on the slime,
While Fate above her fingered with her urn.

* * * * * * *

Then from the tug beside them came the hail:
"They have none at the stores, nor at the dock,
Nor at the quarry, so I tried the gaol.
They thought they had, but it was out of stock.

"So then I telephoned to town; they say
They've sent an engine with some to the pier;
I did not leave till it was on its way,
A tug is waiting there to bring it here:

"It can't be here, though, for an hour or more;
I've lost an hour in trying, as it is.
For want of thought commend me to the shore.
You'd think they'd know their river's ways by this."

"So there is nothing for it but to wait,"
The Captain answered, fuming.   "Until then,
We'd better go to dinner, Mr. Mate."
The cook brought dinner forward to the men.

*   *   *   *   *   *   *

Another hour of prison loitered by;
The strips of sunlight stiffened at the port,
But still the digger made the pellets fly,
Paying no heed to his companions' sport,

While they, about him, spooning at their tins,
Asked if he dug because he found it cold,
Or whether it was penance for his sins,
Or hope of treasure in the forward hold.

He grinned and cursed, but did not cease to pick,
His sweat dropped from him when he bent his head,
His knife-blade quarried down, till with a click
Its grinded thinness snapped against the lead.

Then, dully rising, brushing back his sweat,
He asked his fellows for another knife.
"Never," they said; "man, what d'ye hope to get?"
"Nothing," he said, "except a chance for life."

"Havers," they said, and one among them growled,
"You'll get no knife from any here to break.
You've dug the manhole since the door was fouled,
And now your knife's broke, quit, for Jesus' sake."

But one, who smelt a bargain, changed his tone,
Offering a sheath-knife for the task in hand
At twenty times its value, as a loan
To be repaid him when they reached the land.

And there was jesting at the lender's greed
And mockery at the digger's want of sense,
Closing with such a bargain without need,
Since in an hour the tug would take them thence.

But "Right," the digger said. The deal was made
He took the borrowed knife, and sitting down
Gourged at the channelled solder with the blade,
Saying, "Let be, it's better dig than drown."

And nothing happened for a while; the heat
Grew in the otuffy room, the sunlight slid,
Flies buzzed about and jostled at the meat,
The knife-blade clicked upon the manhole lid:

And one man said, "She takes a hell of time
Bringing the blaster," and another snored;
One, between pipe-puffs, hummed a smutty rhyme,
One, who was weaving, thudded with his sword.

It was as though the ship were in a dream,
Caught in a magic ocean, calm like death,
Tranced, till a presence should arise and gleam,
Making the waters conscious with her breath.

It was so drowsy that the river's cries,
Roaring aloud their ever-changing tune,
Came to those sailors like the drone of flies,
Filling with sleep the summer afternoon.

So that they slept, or, if they spoke, it was
Only to worry lest the tug should come:
Such power upon the body labour has
That prison seemed a blessed rest to some,

Till one man leaning at the port-hole, stared,
Checking his yawning at the widest stretch,
Then blinked and swallowed, while he muttered, scared,
"That blasting-cotton takes an age to fetch."

Then swiftly passing from the port he went
Up and then down the fo'c'sle till he stayed,
Fixed at the port-hole with his eyes intent,
Round-eyed and white, as if he were afraid,

And muttered as he stared, "My God! she is.
She's deeper than she was, she's settling down.
That palm-tree top was steady against this,
And now I see the quay below the town.

"Look here at her. She's sinking in her tracks.
She's going down by inches as she stands,
The water's darker and it stinks like flax,
Her going down is churning up the sands."

And instantly a panic took the crew,
Even the digger blenched; his knife-blade's haste
Cutting the solder witnessed that he knew
Time on the brink with not a breath to waste.

While far away the tugboat at the quay
Under her drooping pennon waited still
For that explosive which would set them free,
Free, with the world a servant to their will.

Then from a boat beside them came a blare,
Urging that tugboat to be quick; and men
Shouted to stir her from her waiting there,
"Hurry the blast, and get us out of pen.

"She's going down. She's going down, man! Quick!"
The tugboat did not stir, no answer came;
They saw her tongue-like pennon idly lick
Clear for an instant, lettered with her name.

Then droop again. The engine had not come,
The blast had not arrived. The prisoned hands
Saw her still waiting though their time had come,
Their ship was going down among the sands,

Going so swiftly now, that they could see
The banks arising as she made her bed;
Full of sick sound she settled deathward, she
Gurgled and shook, the digger picked the lead.

And, as she paused to take a final plunge,
Prone like a half-tide rock, the men on deck
Jumped to their boats and left, ere like a sponge
The river's rotten heart absorbed the wreck;

And on the perilous instant ere Time struck,
The digger's work was done, the lead was cleared,
He cast the manhole up; below it muck
Floated, the hold was full, the water leered.

All of his labour had but made a hole
By which to leap to death; he saw black dust
Float on the bubbles of that brimming bowl,
He drew a breath and took his life in trust,

And plunged head foremost into that black pit,
Where floating cargo bumped against the beams.
He groped a choking passage blind with grit,
The roaring in his ears was shot with screams.

So, with a bursting heart and roaring ears
He floundered in that sunk ship's inky womb,
Drowned in deep water for what seemed like years,
Buried alive and groping through the tomb,

Till suddenly the beams against his back
Gave, and the water on his eyes was bright;
He shot up through a hatchway foul with wrack
Into clean air and life and dazzling light,

And striking out, he saw the fo'c'sle gone,
Vanished, below the water, and the mast
Standing columnar from the sea; it shone
Proud, with its colours flying to the last.

And all about, a many-wrinkled tide
Smoothed and erased its eddies, wandering chilled,
Like glutted purpose, trying to decide
If its achievement had been what it willed.

And men in boats were there; they helped him in.
He gulped for breath and watched that patch of smooth,
Shaped like the vessel, wrinkle into grin,
Furrow to waves and bare a yellow tooth.

Then the masts leaned until the shroud-screws gave.
All disappeared — her masts, her colours, all.
He saw the yardarms tilting to the grave;
He heard the siren of a tugboat call,

And saw her speeding, foaming at the bow,
Bringing the blast-charge that had come too late.
He heard one shout, "It isn't wanted now."
Time's minute-hand had been the hand of Fate.

Then the boats turned; they brought him to the shore.
Men crowded round him, touched him, and were kind;
The Mate walked with him, silent, to the store.
He said, "We've left the best of us behind."

Then, as he wrung his sodden clothes, the Mate
Gave him a drink of rum, and talked awhile
Of men and ships and unexpected Fate;
And darkness came and cloaked the river's guile,

So that its huddled hurry was not seen,
Only made louder, till the full moon climbed
Over the forest, floated, and was queen.
Within the town a temple-belfry chimed.

Then, upon silent pads, a tiger crept
Down to the river-brink, and crouching there
Watched it intently, till you thought he slept
But for his ghastly eye and stiffened hair.

Then, trembling at a lust more fell than his,
He roared and bounded back to coverts lone,
Where, among moonlit beauty, slaughter is,
Filling the marvellous night with myriad groan.

GLOSSARY

Abaft the beam. — That half of a ship included between her amidship section and the taffrail. (For ' taffrail,' *see* below.)

Abel Brown. — An unquotable sea-song.

Advance-note. — A note for one month's wages issued to sailors on their signing a ship's articles.

Belaying-pins. — Bars of iron or hard wood to which running rigging may be secured or *belayed*.

Belaying-pins, from their handiness and peculiar club-shape, are sometimes used as bludgeons.

Bloody. — An intensive derived from the substantive ' blood,' a name applied to the Bucks, Scowrers, and Mohocks of the seventeenth and eighteenth centuries.

Blue Peter. — A blue and white flag hoisted at the foretrucks of ships about to sail.

Bollard. — From **böl** or **bole**, the round trunk of a tree. A phallic or ' sparklet '-shaped ornament of the dockside, of assistance to mariners in warping into or out of dock.

Bonded Jacky. — Negro-head tobacco or sweet cake.

Bull of Barney. — A beast mentioned in an unquotable sea-proverb.

Bumpkin. — An iron bar (projecting out-board from the ship's side) to which the lower and topsail brace blocks are sometimes hooked.

Cape Horn fever. — The illness proper to malingerers.

Catted. — Said of an anchor when weighed and secured to the ' cathead.'

Chanty. — A song sung to lighten labour at the capstan sheets, and halliards. The soloist is known as the chanty-man, and is usually a person of some authority in the fo'c's'le. Many chanties are of great beauty and extreme antiquity.

Clipper-bow. — A bow of delicate curves and lines.

Clout. — A rag or cloth. Also a blow : — ' I fetched him a clout i' the lug.'

Crimp. — A sort of scoundrelly land-shark preying upon sailors.

D.B.S. — Distressed British Sailor. A term applied to those who are invalided home from foreign ports.

Dungaree. — A cheap, rough, thin cloth (generally blue or brown), woven, I am told, of coco-nut fibre.

Forward or Forrard. — Towards the bows.

Fo'c's'le (Forecastle). — The deck-house or living-room of the crew. The word is often used to indicate the crew, or those members of it described by passengers as the ' common sailors.'

Fore-stay. — A powerful wire rope supporting the foremast forward.

Gaskets. — Ropes or plaited lines used to secure the sails in furling.

Goneys. — Albatrosses.

Guffy. — A marine or jolly.

Gullies. — Sea-gulls, Cape Horn pigeons, etc.

Heave and pawl. — A cry of encouragement at the capstan.

Hooker. — A periphrasis for ship, I suppose from a ship's carrying hooks or anchors.

Jack or Jackstay. — A slender iron rail running along the upper portions of the yards in some ships.

Leeward. — Pronounced ' looard.' That quarter to which the wind blows.

Mainsail haul. — An order in tacking ship bidding ' swing the main-yards.' To loot, steal, or ' acquire.'

Main-shrouds. — Ropes, usually wire, supporting lateral strains upon the mainmast.

Mollies. — Molly-hawks, or Fulmar petrels. Wide-winged dusky sea-fowls, common in high latitudes, oily to taste, gluttonous. Great fishers and garbage-eaters.

Port Mahon Baboon, or **Port Mahon Soger.** — I have been unable to discover either the origin of these insulting epithets or the reasons for the peculiar bitterness with which they sting the marine recipient. They are older than Dana (*circe* 1840).

An old merchant sailor, now dead, once told me that Port Mahon was that godless city from which the Ark set sail, in which case the name may have some traditional connection with that evil 'Mahoun' or 'Mahu,' prince of darkness, mentioned by Shakespeare and some of our older poets.

The real Port Mahon, a fine harbour in Minorca, was taken by the French, from Admiral Byng, in the year 1756.

I think that the phrases originated at the time of Byng's consequent trial and execution.

Purchase. — *See* ' Tackle.'

Quidding. — Tobacco-chewing.

Sails. — The sail-maker.

Santa Cruz. — A brand of rum.

Scantling. — Planks.

Soger. — A laggard, malingerer, or hang-back. To loaf or skulk or work Tom Cox's Traverse.

Spunyarn. — A three-strand line spun out of old rope-yarn knotted together. Most sailing-ships carry a spunyarn winch, and the spinning of such yarn is a favourite occupation in fine weather.

Stirrup. — A short rope supporting the foot-rope on which the sailors stand when aloft on the yards.

Tack. — To stay or 'bout ship. A reach to windward. The weather lower corner of a course.

Tackle. — Pronounced **taykle.** A combination of pulleys for obtaining of artificial power.

Taffrail. — The rail or bulwark round the sternmost end of a ship's poop or after-deck.

Trick. — The ordinary two-hour spell at the wheel or on the look-out.

Windward or **Weather.** — That quarter from which the wind blows.